COUNTRY
GARDENS

the
Edible Garden

COUNTRY
GARDENS

the
Edible Garden

GROW YOUR OWN VEGETABLES, FRUITS & HERBS
NO MATTER WHERE YOU LIVE

weldon**owen**

Planning, Planting & Cultivating

Spring

Summer

Fall

Raising food has never been easier—or more fun. And growing food right outside your back door means harvesting is more convenient than ever.

You can grow food from seeds or plant seedlings in your garden, and once you raise a few of your own crops (and see how easy and tasty they are), you'll want to expand your garden year after year. With the diverse selection of fruit and vegetable varieties available today, you can delve into a wide, flavorful world of heirloom and specialty produce. With hundreds of tomatoes to choose from, don't settle for tasteless, juiceless, nondescript ones. New, improved, and disease-resistant varieties make growing fruits and vegetables easier than ever before. And you don't need a lot of space to raise them. Container gardening means that anyone—with or without a yard—can grow strawberries, lettuces, herbs, and even small fruit trees in containers. Plus, you can place containers conveniently near the kitchen. What can taste more vibrant than fresh basil or rosemary added to hot pasta with good olive oil? Gardeners who grow organic food know what type of soil and amendments the food has been growing in. If you choose to raise food without pesticides or herbicides, you can be confident in the quality of your food. The delicious results are healthful and safe food ... and the fresh goodness will shine through.

James A. Baggett
Editor, *The Edible Garden*

CHAPTER 1

Planning, Planting & Cultivating

CLIMATE AND SEASONS

Take cues from climate and seasons when choosing which fruits, vegetables, and herbs to plant and when to plant them.

001
STAY COOL

Cool-season vegetables grow best when temperatures range between 40°F and 75°F (4–24°C). In most areas, these can be planted two to four weeks before the last spring frost because the seeds germinate best in cool soil. These crops often develop edible roots, stems, leaves, or buds. Cool-season crops stop producing in early summer when temperatures range above 80°F (27°C); however, in regions where nights remain cool, seeds can be sown every two weeks. This method, called succession planting, ensures a bountiful harvest from spring to fall.

002
KNOW YOUR COOL-SEASON CROPS

These vegetables love cool soil and cool temperatures. Plant them in early spring.

Asparagus	Carrot	Kale	Pea
Beet	Cauliflower	Kohlrabi	Potato
Broccoli	Celery	Leek	Radish
Brussels sprouts	Chard	Lettuce	Rhubarb
Cabbage	Collards	Onion	Rutabaga
	Garlic	Parsnip	Spinach

003
KEEP WARM

Warm-season vegetables originated in tropical climates. These crops develop edible fruits, are killed by frost, and won't perform well when temperatures fall below 50°F (10°C). Wait until about two weeks after the average last frost date in your area to plant warm-season crops.

004
KNOW YOUR WARM-SEASON CROPS

Heat makes these vegetables produce fruit. Plant them in the garden after the last chance of frost passes.

Artichoke	Peanut
Bean	Pepper
Corn	Squash
Cucumber	Sweet Potato
Eggplant	Tomatillo
Melon	Tomato
Okra	

005 GROW IN TWO SEASONS

Relative to climate, vegetables are divided into two different groups: cool season and warm season. Gardeners in most regions can successfully grow both types of crops.

006
UNDERSTAND MICROCLIMATES

Planting trees and shrubs in a microclimate can protect tender fruit crops. A microclimate is the climate in a small area that is warmer or colder than the climate around it. Your house and other buildings create microclimates by absorbing heat during the day and radiating it into the landscape at night. The south side of a building is the warmest microclimate. Others include balconies and rooftops, fences, walls, large rocks, patios, driveways, and sidewalks. Keep in mind that cold, dry winds may mitigate any heat gain.

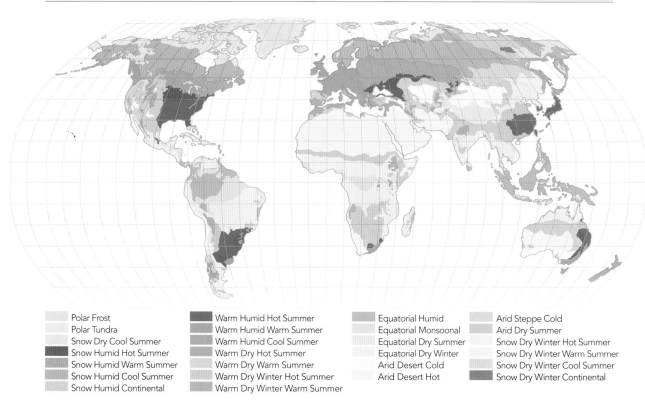

Polar Frost	Warm Humid Hot Summer	Equatorial Humid	Arid Steppe Cold
Polar Tundra	Warm Humid Warm Summer	Equatorial Monsoonal	Arid Dry Summer
Snow Dry Cool Summer	Warm Humid Cool Summer	Equatorial Dry Summer	Snow Dry Winter Hot Summer
Snow Humid Hot Summer	Warm Dry Hot Summer	Equatorial Dry Winter	Snow Dry Winter Warm Summer
Snow Humid Warm Summer	Warm Dry Warm Summer	Arid Desert Cold	Snow Dry Winter Cool Summer
Snow Humid Cool Summer	Warm Dry Winter Hot Summer	Arid Desert Hot	Snow Dry Winter Continental
Snow Humid Continental	Warm Dry Winter Warm Summer		

007
KNOW YOUR CLIMATE

With a few exceptions—such as the tundra and the most severely dry desert conditions—it's possible to do some kind of gardening nearly anywhere in the world.

The most important first step in planting a garden is to thoroughly understand the environmental factors that will come to bear on plants in your part of the world. Climate consists of three elements. The main climate—whether it is arid, warm, or equatorial or snowy, for instance. The second is the amount of precipitation during any given season. And the third is the range of temperatures during any given season. You will obviously have the most success as a gardener by choosing plants that are right for your particular climate and for their resistance to disease and pests in your region.

008
BE FRUITFUL

Fruit trees and shrubs are grown as perennial plants and are particular when it comes to climate. Cold temperatures thwart the growth of plants roots, stems, and leaves and bring about a late spring frost that will nip tender buds. Frost might not damage the plant, but it will kill buds, preventing fruit from forming. However, most fruit trees need a specific amount of heat to produce fruit while having a low tolerance of high temperatures. Most fruiting plants have a wide adaptation to temperature and produce fruit in all but extremely hot- or cold-summer areas. For reliable crops, rely on plants that are hardy in your particular climate.

009
GARDEN WHERE YOU LIVE

Climate in each area consists of varying weather patterns: temperature, wind, sunlight, frost, rain, snow, and humidity. The effects that climate can have on gardens are complex.

Gardeners have a close relationship with weather; gardens don't grow without light, rain, and heat. In spring, the morning sun on a rain-soaked garden is a welcome author of blooms. But in a summer drought, the sun is cruel when it leaves earth cracked, petals scorched, and leaves wilted.

Savvy gardeners adapt and look for ways to overcome obstacles. Dry desert gardens require conservative water use and native plants. In cold-winter areas, mulch helps plants survive dramatic temperature swings of freeze-thaw cycles that can injure or destroy plants.

Gardeners who know they cannot change weather strive to understand, gauge, and prepare for extremes.

The best tool for weather-conscious gardeners is a well-adjusted attitude. Sharpen your senses of awe, humor, and defiance, knowing that weather is an ally and a threat, and don't let it dampen your gardening spirit.

GOOD EARTH

Every delicious tomato, strawberry, and carrot begins with properly prepared soil. Invest time and effort in preparing soil and you'll reap edible dividends.

010
GET THE DIRT ON SOIL

Soil is the storehouse for nutrients, water, and oxygen; healthy soil promotes healthy plants. There are three soil types: sand, silt, and clay. Soils are almost always a mixture of sand, silt, and clay. Soils made of sand have the largest particles and the largest amount of space for water and air to move through the soil. Sandy soil drains quickly, taking nutrients with it, which is why it's usually low in fertility. Silt is composed of tiny rounded particles; it drains more slowly than sandy soil and retains more nutrients. Clay particles are microscopic, and an ounce of soil may contain millions of clay particles, which often pack together so tightly that roots have a hard time making their way through the soil.

The ideal growing medium is loamy soil, which consists of 40 percent sand, 40 percent silt, and 20 percent clay. Loam holds moisture and nutrients yet has pore space for air, water, and roots. Determining soil texture is as easy as moistening ½ cup (45 g) of soil with water. Roll it into a ball, and try forming it into a ribbon between your hands.

011 DO THE SQUEEZE TEST

CLAY SOIL (A) If soil packs together and easily forms a ribbon, the soil is clay or has a high clay component. It is sticky and will probably stain your skin. If the soil ribbon feels smooth instead of sticky, it is probably silty clay. If it is gritty, it is sandy clay.

LOAM (B) If soil ribbon holds together but is loose and tends to crumble, it contains a high amount of silt, sand, or organic matter. It is most likely a loam soil.

SANDY SOIL (C) If soil will not hold together, breaking apart regardless of how much water you apply, it is a sandy soil. It is gritty, and you will feel individual grains.

012
ASSESS YOUR SOIL NUTRIENTS

All plants source carbon, hydrogen, and oxygen from the atmosphere and water and mine the soil for nitrogen, phosphorus, potassium, and other important elements.

A soil test can pinpoint nutrient deficiencies and excesses, pH values, and include recommendations for improving your soil. Most county extension services will perform soil tests or provide referrals to commercial labs. Test your soil if plants are showing poor or stunted growth over the course of the growing season.

013
DIG A HOLE TO TEST DRAINAGE

Drainage is how much and how fast water moves through the soil. Soil with good drainage has a good supply of oxygen, which is vital to root and plant health. Clay soils drain slowly, and sandy soils drain rapidly. To test your soil, grab a shovel and head to the garden.

STEP 1 Dig a hole 12 inches (30 cm) deep and 8 to 12 inches (20–30 cm) in diameter in soil that is moist but not soggy.

STEP 2 Fill the hole with water. Allow it to drain, and refill it 12 hours later, noting the time.

STEP 3 Time the drainage. If it drains well, all the water will be gone in two to three hours. If it takes 10 or more hours to empty, it is poorly drained, and most plants will struggle to survive in that area.

014 BOOST SOIL NUTRIENTS

As plants grow, they harvest nutrients from soil. It's a gardener's job to replenish nutrients so the soil can continue to provide all the elements necessary for plant growth. The nutrients that plants use in large quantities that might be deficient are nitrogen (chemical symbol N), phosphorus (P), and potassium (K).

015
DIAGNOSE DEFICIENCIES

Plants use leaves, stems, and growth habit to communicate general well-being. Sometimes poor growth, discolored leaves, or dead foliage indicate low nutrient levels in the soil. If your plants exhibit the following deficiency symptoms, take a soil test.

NITROGEN DEFICIENCY
Growth is slow and stunted. Leaves begin to yellow, starting with the oldest, and then moving to the younger leaves.

PHOSPHORUS DEFICIENCY
Growth is slow, bearing few flowers or fruits, and displaying unusually dark green or purple foliage.

POTASSIUM DEFICIENCY
The plant shows weak stems and shriveled fruit, and scorch marks on the margins of the oldest leaves.

016
READ THE LABEL

Fertilizers are labeled according to the percentage of N, P, and K they contain. A fertilizer label will show three numbers separated by hyphens, such as 10-10-10. The first number represents the percentage of nitrogen in the fertilizer. The second and third numbers represent phosphorus and potassium, respectively.

018
CHOOSE A NUTRIENT SOURCE FOR YOUR GARDEN

Synthetic fertilizers are available as granular products or liquids. There are many different N-P-K combinations and even crop-specific formulations.

BLOOD MEAL This dried, powdered blood collected from beef processing facilities has a formulation of 12-0-0 and is a rich source of nitrogen.

COMPOST Made of decomposed plant parts, you can DIY at home, or purchase it in bulk at garden centers. Most commercial compost has a chemical formulation of 1.5-1-1. Compost contains nutrients and has microbes that improve soil structure and suppress disease.

COTTONSEED MEAL This by-product of cotton processing has a formulation of 6-3-2.

COVER CROPS These are planted in fall or early spring and tilled into soil two to three weeks before planting. Annual ryegrass and oats are two popular cover crops and add valuable nitrogen to soil while improving soil structure.

FISH EMULSION This partially decomposed blend of finely pulverized fish has a formulation of 4-2-2. The odor can be offensive during application, but it dissipates in a day or two.

Test Garden Tip
017
BLANKET YOUR GARDEN

A layer of straw mulch around plants has many benefits: It prevents weeds, slows soil moisture evaporation, and slowly decomposes, improving soil structure.

019 ADD A LAYER OF COMPOST

Well-made compost is packed with more nutrients and beneficial microorganisms than many other soil amendments. Buy compost at a garden center, or if you have a few feet of space, you can make your own (see #021).

020
PICK A COMPOSTING METHOD

Here are a few common composting methods and bins; choose the best for you.

HOLDING UNITS A good choice for apartment dwellers and gardeners with limited space, these units do not require turning. Layers of green and brown materials are simply piled in the unit, moistened, and then left to decompose.

TURNING UNITS Designed to promote aeration, turning units may be either a series of bins or a structure that rotates, such as a ball or barrel.

HEAPS A compost heap is simply a carefully layered pile of compostable material, preferably located in part shade and on soil or a pallet if poor drainage is a concern. They do not require a bin or structure.

SHEET COMPOSTING With this method, a thin layer of materials, such as leaves or other landscape debris, is worked into garden soil in the fall. By spring, the material will be broken down.

TRENCH COMPOSTING This method involves digging a trench and filling it with thick layers of green and brown compost materials, then topping with soil. It is especially beneficial for vegetable gardens that are arranged in rows.

021 MAKE YOUR OWN COMPOST

Make a compost heap by spreading a 3-inch (8-cm) layer of brown material on the soil. Top with a 3-inch (8-cm) layer of green material. Continue layering as materials become available, and water the pile until it is as moist as a wrung-out sponge. Turn the pile once every two weeks.

STEP 1 BROWN MATERIAL Leaves, dried grass, small wood chips, twigs, soil, and shredded newspaper contribute valuable carbon and microorganisms to the pile.

STEP 2 GREEN MATERIAL Fresh grass clippings, kitchen scraps from fruits and vegetables, and garden waste provide compost with valuable nitrogen.

STEP 3 WATER Add water to the pile to encourage bacteria growth and decomposition. Turn the pile every two weeks, and you'll have nutrient-rich humus in a few short months.

DESIGN A GARDEN

Have you been bitten by the gardening bug but aren't sure how to get growing?

022 PLAN YOUR GARDEN

When it comes to planning your garden, first choose where you will plant, then decide what you want to grow, how you will plant—seeds, seedlings, or both—and when.

Determining the size of your garden is a matter of how much you want to harvest, the amount of space you have, and how much work you're willing to do. For a beginner, it's prudent to keep a garden modest; you can always enlarge it later.

Traditional garden plots arrange plants in rows, and gardeners use the space between them for access. Gardening in small beds is gaining in popularity. Garden beds are divided into blocks, each 3 to 4 feet (0.91–1.2 m) wide with permanent paths between them to tend plants by leaning in, without compacting garden soil. Raised beds are preferred by many gardeners because they keep gardens tidy. They also allow for raising the ground level with ideal soil when filled with a custom blend of topsoil, compost, and other soil amendments. Other options include adding edible plants to an existing bed with ornamental plants, or using containers on a patio, balcony, or deck.

Which vegetables, herbs, and fruits to plant in your garden depends on what you like to eat. Raise the foods you and your family will use and enjoy the most. Choose to buy a four- or six-pack of plants at a garden center or to sow seeds; seeds offer far more varieties than you'll find as seedlings. Planting time varies by climate and type of vegetable, herb, or fruit. The first and last average frost dates in your region determine the length of the average growing season and which crops you can successfully plant and harvest between spring and fall.

023 START FROM SEED

Growing seedlings is a two-part process. Sowing seeds and encouraging them to germinate (sprout) come first, followed by growing the seedlings into sturdy young plants ready for life in the garden. Seed packets instruct how early to start plants, usually 4 to 10 weeks before their outdoor planting season begins. Plants labeled "hardy" can be transplanted into the garden after the last frost. Others must wait until night temperatures reach 50°F (10°C) or be protected by a cloche or mini greenhouse. Fruit plants are rarely started from seed. Tree fruits, such as apples, and most berries usually are started from nursery-grown transplants.

024 SOW AND GERMINATE

Growing seedlings is a two-part process. Sowing seeds and encouraging them to germinate is the first step.

CONTAINERS Plant in new or clean pots or containers with good drainage. Sow seeds of plants that transplant with difficulty in individual biodegradable peat pots so they can be transplanted in the pot.

SOIL Fill pots with premoistened soilless seed-starting mix. A formula containing peat or coir, and perlite or vermiculite, is best for plants that will be indoors for at least six weeks.

MOISTURE Cover pots with clear plastic or a tent of sheet plastic to maintain even moisture in the seed-starting mix until seeds germinate. Gently water with a mister, or place pots in a watertight container and pour 1 to 2 inches (2.5–5 cm) of water into the container. Water will naturally travel into the dry soil. Remove the container from the water tray as soon as the top of the soil is moist.

HEAT Warm soil and adequate moisture trigger seedlings to germinate. Under ideal soil temperatures, most seeds will germinate within one week. Place containers on a heating mat, a heating pad set on low, or a tepid radiator to speed germination.

LIGHT Follow instructions on seed packets. Some seeds require moderate light; some need darkness to germinate.

TIMING Check containers every few days. When most of the seedlings have emerged, the second stage begins.

025 GROW AND TRANSPLANT

The second step of growing seedlings is nourishing them into sturdy young plants.

LIGHT Once seeds have germinated, remove covers and place pots in bright light. A sunny sill is fine for seedlings that will go outdoors in four weeks. Plants that will be indoors for six weeks or more do better under grow lights that are lit for 14 to 16 hours a day.

MOISTURE Keep seed-starting mix evenly damp. Watering from the bottom is best.

SPACE Thin seedlings as they become crowded. If need be, set up a small fan in the room to keep air moving among the plants.

POTTING As seedlings in flats become crowded, transplant them into individual 2-inch (5-cm) pots filled with sterile potting mix. Large plants might need to be transplanted into a larger pot before being planted outside. Once seedling height is three times the diameter of the pot, it's time to move it to a larger pot.

FERTILIZER Every two weeks, fertilize seedlings that will be indoors for six weeks or more. Use soluble all-purpose fertilizer (20-20-20) at half strength.

HARDENING OFF One week before transplanting seedlings into the garden, place them outside, ideally on a cloudy, windless day that's above 50°F (10°C), for a few hours. Gradually extend the amount of time they are outdoors each day until they're ready.

026 START SEEDS, STEP-BY-STEP

Plant seeds indoors six to eight weeks before you plan to plant them outside. Tomatoes and peppers are some of the most popular edibles to start from seeds. These easy-to-grow plants germinate readily and grow rapidly.

STEP 1 Choose a container. Start seeds in any type of container that drains readily. Peat pots and peat pellets are especially easy to use because they can be planted directly in the garden. You also can recycle nursery containers; be sure to clean them well before seeding.

STEP 2 Add potting soil. Unless you are using peat pellets, it is necessary to add potting soil to your container. A seed-starting potting mix is ideal, but you also can use an all-purpose potting soil. Quick drainage is essential, and a slow-release fertilizer is a good addition. Use a straightedge, such as a small ruler, to level the potting soil, being very careful not to compact it.

STEP 3 Plant and water seeds. Using cardstock folded into a trough, drop two or three seeds into each pot or pellet. Planting depth depends on the plant. Some seeds are planted ½ inch (12 mm) deep while others grow best when they are planted just 1⁄8 inch (3 mm) deep. Using a spray bottle, mist the soil daily until seedlings emerge.

STEP 4 Place seedlings under light. After the seedlings germinate, move them to a bright location. Fluorescent lights are ideal. Use two bulbs—one cool white and one warm white—to provide ample light for fourteen or so hours per day.

027
TAKE THE TEMPERATURE

Purchase a soil thermometer next time you're at a garden center. These cool-season vegetables germinate from seed at the prescribed soil temperatures.

40°F (4°C)
Arugula, Fava Bean, Kale, Lettuce, Parsnip, Pea, Radicchio, Radish, Spinach

50°F (10°C)
Chinese Cabbage, Leek, Onion, Swiss Chard, Turnip

60°F (16°C)
Beet, Broccoli, Brussels Sprout, Cabbage, Carrot, Cauliflower

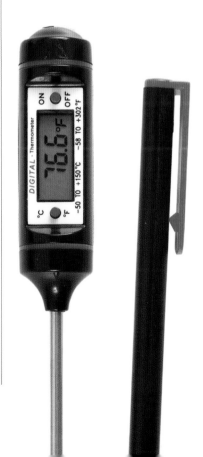

028
RAISE IT UP

With small monetary investment and a few hours of work, you can build a raised bed over poor soil—a practical solution for small gardens and urban and rooftop gardens where planting space is at a premium.

CONSTRUCTION

SIZE To prevent walking in a raised bed, build it no wider than 4 feet (1.2 m). Bed length is dependent on site. Opt for short beds with 2-foot (61-cm) paths between to eliminate walking around a long bed. The ideal beds are 12 to 24 inches (30–61 cm) tall, which allows adequate rooting space and easy construction. Taller beds require retaining walls with foundations.

MATERIALS Stone, brick, cement block, and untreated wood are fine building materials for raised beds. Kits are also available.

SOIL Before filling raised bed with quality topsoil, loosen ground-level soil by rototilling it or turning it over with a spade. Then mix the native soil with topsoil to fill the raised bed.

MAINTENANCE

WATER Raised beds dry out faster than traditional gardens. Spread a 2-inch (5-cm) layer of organic mulch around plants to help hold soil moisture. Be prepared to water them frequently.

AVOID COMPACTION Never walk on a raised bed. The weight will quickly destroy soil structure.

END OF SEASON Disease-free plant parts can be tilled or spaded into the soil. Mix in additional organic matter to add more nutrients and improve soil structure. Over time, soil may improve so that little if any tilling is necessary.

029 BUILD A RAISED BED

What's not to love about raised-bed gardening? These tidy, efficient gardens rise above slow-draining, compacted soil and reduce the need to bend and stoop as you care for plants. Build a raised bed in an afternoon with these easy instructions.

STEP 1 Select a site and remove sod. For ease of construction, choose a level site. Also pay attention to sunlight. Most edibles require at least 8 hours of direct sunlight per day. Delineate edges of the bed with white marking paint, and use a sharp spade to skim the sod off the site. If this is your first garden, start small—a 4×4-foot (1.2×1.2 m) bed will provide plenty of planting space.

STEP 2 Construct the frame. Build the raised-bed frame using a raised-bed kit, available at home improvement stores and on the Internet, or make your own using untreated lumber. A simple design involves using 4×4s (1.2×1.2 m) for corner posts and attaching 2×6s (5×15 cm) to form side rails.

STEP 3 Loosen the soil. Set the course for a well-drained bed by loosening the native soil. Most likely compacted during construction, native soil has the potential to thwart good drainage of the raised bed by not allowing water to percolate into the ground below the bed. Use a sharp spade to turn soil to a depth of about 8 inches (20 cm).

STEP 4 Add soil. Fill the new bed with high-quality, nutrient-rich soil. Mix in a generous amount of compost and other amendments if a soil test indicates they are necessary. Garden centers stock bagged products that contain ample nutrients and have excellent drainage for raised-bed gardening.

STEP 5 Mix it together. Using a small tiller or spade, combine the topsoil, soil amendments, and a few inches (centimeters) of native soil for a uniform mixture.

STEP 6 Plant your garden. Raised beds are excellent for growing plants from seeds or transplants. Even perennial plants, such as blueberries or brambles, can be grown in raised beds.

030
ENRICH
THE SOIL

Little preparation, other than adding compost, is needed when vegetables are planted in existing landscape beds to form an edible landscape.

PLANTING TIME

New landscape beds and vegetable plots require just a few hours of time, some muscle power, and compost to prep for planting. Here's a quick summary to guide you through the process.

031 MAKE A PLANTING BED

Planting seeds or transplants in the garden begins with preparing the soil.

REMOVE SOD Your soon-to-be vegetable garden is most likely blanketed with turfgrass. Begin by skimming away the sod and as many roots as possible. There are several ways to accomplish this. A low-cost option is to use a sharp shovel to slice under the grass, cutting below the sod's 2-to-3 inch- (5–8-cm-) deep root zone. Sod can also be removed with a sod cutter. Rent this small machine at a home improvement store for the day. If you have four to eight weeks, smother the grass by covering it with sections of newspaper and topping the paper with wood mulch. Water the mulch well to prevent the paper from blowing. The grass will die and the newspaper will decompose. Till or turn the soil, incorporate compost, and plant seeds or transplants.

CHECK SOIL DRYNESS Before tilling or turning the soil, check soil moisture. Press a handful of soil in your fist and squeeze. If the soil readily crumbles, you can till or turn the soil. If water oozes out when you squeeze, wait a few more days and check the soil again.

ADD COMPOST Spread a 2-inch (5-cm) layer of well-decomposed compost over the garden and mix it in the soil to a depth of about 8 inches (20 cm). Add compost annually in spring or fall.

LOOSEN SOIL Topsoil in a vegetable garden should have a fine texture and be free of large clods so sprouts can grow through the soil surface and water can seep into the root zone. Use a tiller or long-handle spade to turn the soil and break up clods. Then use a stiff garden rake to smooth the soil.

032 READ YOUR SEED PACKETS

Much of the information you need for planting is on the back of a seed packet: plant spacing and planting depth as well as mature plant size, and days from planting time to harvest ("days to maturity"). Seed packets also detail special treatments the seeds might require prior to planting, such as soaking in water to soften hard outer coverings. The first sunny day after a long winter might spur you to begin planting, but while the air temperature might be warm, the soil temperature is probably still cool.

033
GROW IN ROWS

The most common method to plant seeds is in straight narrow rows. Use a hoe or tool handle to make a depression in loose soil for the planting furrow. To make a straight row, run a plumb line from a stake at either end of the planting bed. Place the seeds in the furrow, spacing them and covering with loose soil as directed on the seed packet. Firm the covered row with your hand and water gently.

Another way to plant seeds is in wide rows, which offer efficiency in small spaces by eliminating pathways. Wide rows should be no more than 4 feet (1.2 m) across. Sprinkle seeds on the bed; once most of the seeds have germinated, thin any crowded seedlings to proper spacing.

Some vining crops, such as melons and pumpkins, are traditionally grown on mounds of soil called hills. Create a 3-foot-(91-cm-) diameter, flat-top mound on heavy or sandy soil. Plant five or six evenly spaced seeds per hill. Thin all but the strongest few seedlings to the proper spacing.

034
NURTURE YOUR SEEDLINGS

Nature throws a bevy of diverse weather conditions at tender young seedlings in spring. There are a few things you can do to counter weather extremes.

BE WATER SMART Seedlings need about 1 inch (2.5 cm) of water per week. If it does not rain, water them gently.

ADD A LAYER OF MULCH After plants develop a second set of leaves, spread a 1-inch (2.5-cm) layer of finely shredded bark, leaves, or other organic mulch around plants. Keep mulch away from tender stems.

THIN PLANTS Thin seedlings by cutting off the weakest seedlings at ground level. Thin established plants by snipping them or gently pulling them out if doing so will not disturb the root system of nearby plants.

CONSIDER ROW COVERS Made of lightweight fabric resembling

cheesecloth, floating row covers let sunlight, water, and air through while blocking insects and keeping the plants slightly warmer. Some vegetables, such as lettuce and broccoli, can be grown to maturity under row covers. If warm temperatures are expected, open the row covers to cool the plants. Vegetables that are flowering need to be uncovered and available to insects for pollination.

WATER SMART

How much to water, when to water, and how to water all depend on garden soil, weather, and the edibles you grow.

035 ADD WATER

Watering, like most garden chores, is not a one-size-fits-all kind of practice.

TAKE CUES FROM THE SOIL How much and how fast soil can absorb water depends on the relative amounts of sand, silt, and clay it contains. Mixing compost and other organic matter into clay or sandy soils helps compensate for the weaknesses of both.

WEATHER CONSIDERATIONS Weather figures prominently into watering calculations. If nature delivers 1 inch (2.5 cm) of water or more, you likely will not have to supplement. If not, plan to water, especially early in the season when plants are establishing root systems.

STANDARD FRUIT TREES Trees need a lot of water, and if not supplied by rain, deep irrigation is necessary. Dwarf trees may not need as much water, but they do require a steady supply. A newly planted tree has a root spread of up to 2 square feet (61 sq. cm) and needs a minimum of 2 to 4 gallons (8–15 L) of water a week.

036 LISTEN TO YOUR GARDEN

There are two ways plants indicate they need water long before they start to wilt. A water-hungry plant's foliage may look dull or stems may not stand as tall or look as vibrant. Scratch the soil 1 to 2 inches (2.5–5 cm) below the soil surface. If it is moist, don't water for at least two days. If it is dry, water deeply by soaking the soil to a depth of 6 to 8 inches (15–20 cm) below the surface.

037
CHOOSE A WAY TO WATER

There are several ways to deliver water to your garden.

BASIN IRRIGATION Watering basins are used mainly around fruit trees and shrubs. A ridge of soil is built to contain the water and the basin is filled with water.

SPRINKLERS Hose-end sprinklers and underground-installed sprinklers irrigate a large, densely planted garden at once. They are hard to control in windy areas, and they wet plant leaves, which may lead to disease problems. Choose alternative watering systems if possible.

DRIP IRRIGATION These systems work for any size garden and plants that require constant soil moisture because they apply water slowly, allowing it to seep into the soil. Drip systems do the best watering job without the wet-to-dry fluctuations of other methods, does not wet leaves, and are the ideal solution to watering plants on steep slopes.

038
CONSERVE WATER

Be water smart with these simple water-saving tips.

MULCH IT A 2- to 3-inch (5–8-cm) layer of organic mulch reduces soil-moisture evaporation, keeps soil cooler in summer, and cuts down on weed growth.

ADD ORGANIC MATTER Mix compost, shredded leaves, and other organic soil amendments into the soil to promote water penetration and retention.

TRY CLOSER ROWS Radishes, onions, beets, and carrots are easy to grow in rows 1 foot (30 cm) apart. Stake tomatoes and grow cucumbers on trellises in a densely planted garden.

CHOOSE A FLAT SPACE For the most efficient water penetration, plant on flat terrain.

ELIMINATE WEEDS Weeds compete with plants for water and nutrients. Get rid of them as soon as you spot them.

039
CONSIDER YOUR CROP

Annual plants grow fast and need soil that is consistently moist. Young perennial herbs and young fruiting shrubs and trees will also need frequent water until their roots are established.

ORGANIC GARDENING

Learn how to use organic gardening methods to grow the freshest fruits and vegetables in your garden.

040
GO ORGANIC

One step at a time, you can cultivate a more earth-friendly garden. Here's how.

IMPROVE YOUR SOIL Nurturing soil is the best thing you can do for your garden to enable its health and productivity. Most soils fall short of the ideal, but adding organic materials in the spring, such as compost and chopped leaves, improves any soil. Well-decomposed animal manures are also beneficial soil additions.

MAKE AND USE COMPOST Do it the simple way by collecting organic wastes in a pile or a bin and letting nature take its course. Naturally decomposed waste materials add fertility when dug into soil, creating a loose structure that aids plant growth, encourages soil organisms, and helps retain moisture.

PRACTICE PREVENTION Prevent weeds, pests, and diseases by growing diverse, healthy plants that can resist challenges. Scatter tomato plants around the landscape, and rotate them into different locations each year to minimize the occurrence of disease. Select plant varieties, such as heirlooms or improved hybrids, with proven resistance to disease. Water the garden early in the morning or late in the afternoon, directing water

to the soil and keeping foliage dry. Use mulch to prevent weeds and preserve soil moisture.

CHOOSE RIGHT Provide the sun exposure, soil conditions, moisture levels, and nutrients that plants need. A plant deprived of the light it needs will be more susceptible to disease. Place plants where they'll naturally thrive. Healthier, stronger plants fend off disease or pest attacks and yield more. Avoid pampering plants with too much water or fertilizer.

AVOID CHEMICALS Learn to identify problematic insects and beneficial ones (natural predators), and research solutions to problems. Start with the least-toxic solution. Instead of reaching for a herbicide, pull weeds. Instead of depending on pesticides, minimize and manage pests.

CONSIDER ALTERNATIVE CONTROLS Evaluate a pest or disease problem and the consequences of a management strategy before you act. Some pest problems are mainly cosmetic. If a disease has infected a plant, remove and trash affected plant parts. Banning the use of pesticides allows beneficial insects to deter insect pests. For instance, the Japanese lady beetle feeds on aphids. Instead of pesticides, spray soft-bodied insect pests with a blast of water. Or choose a hot-pepper-and-garlic spray that gives plants armor against aphids, flea beetles, caterpillars,

cabbage worms, and a host of other chewing and sucking insects.

USE EARTH-FRIENDLY SOLUTIONS Explore options among organic fertilizers, pest controls, and disease remedies available from garden centers and mail-order sources. Read product labels to learn how and when to use a product appropriately. Products made for use on ornamental plants may not be safe for use on edibles.

OBSERVE AND ACT A daily walk through the garden with a careful look at leaves, stems, flowers, fruits, and the ground around plants helps you spot signs of problems in time to try effective controls. Most steps taken to manage pests of all kinds require repetition because insects, weeds, and diseases have life cycles. Repeating a method of pest control several times within a month helps minimize the problem and successive generations.

INVITE WILDLIFE Feathered friends will return the favor by eating insect pests in your garden throughout the gardening season. Set out birdhouses, bird feeders in winter and early spring, and birdbaths as further enticement. Also include trees, shrubs, perennials, and annuals that will sustain birds with their favorite berries and seeds as well as shelter. Replace large lawn areas with native plantings, which sustain wildlife.

PESTS, DISEASES & WEEDS

When you think of the word pest your mind might jump to insect pests, but garden pests encompass more than insects. Diseases, animals, and weeds that cause problems for cultivated plants are also considered pests.

041
STRIKE A NATURAL BALANCE

More often than not, insects, diseases, animals, and weeds do not reach pest status because you and nature control their population. Because a healthy garden relies on this intricate interaction between predators and prey, it is essential that you observe pests in your garden before intervening; don't assume an unfamiliar insect is a pest. Weeds, on the other hand, need more vigorous monitoring and often require action. Because weeds readily root in open soil, a 2- to 4-inch (5–10-cm) layer of mulch will thwart seed germination, effectively limiting weed growth most of the season.

042
STAY HEALTHY

The best thing you can do to prevent pests from gaining the upper hand is to grow healthy plants in healthy soil. Research shows that healthy plants have strong immune systems and react to pest outbreaks by releasing chemicals that help sustain them during attack. The soil around newly built homes and in urban areas can be particularly challenging. If the native soil is unmanageable, build raised beds, or garden in containers.

043 MANAGE PESTS

The goal of Integrated Pest Management (IPM) is to solve a problem with the least-toxic effect on the environment. Chemical pest-control methods are the last option and rarely used in IPM. Prevent problems by providing plants with the sun exposure, moisture, and nutrients they require for strong, healthy growth.

IDENTIFY SYMPTOMS AND PESTS As you work in the garden, look for signs of stress or disease, such as yellowing, wilting, puckering, discoloration, and holes in or chewed edges on foliage. For tiny insects, such as mites, hold a piece of white paper under a leaf and tap the leaf and, using a magnifying glass, look for specks crawling on the paper. Use reference books and Internet sources to accurately identify what you find.

MONITOR THE SITUATION If you think a plant has a pest, watch to see what changes take place over the following days or weeks, then decide if control is required.

CHOOSE CONTROL METHODS Start with the least-toxic control methods before advancing to other options, using chemical pest controls as a last result.

KEEP RECORDS AND EVALUATE RESULTS Because insects are usually seasonal, jot down the type of insect, what plant it was on, the type of damage, weather conditions, time of year, and control methods and their effectiveness.

044
BUG OUT
Accurate identification of a
pest is essential for managing
it. Keep an inexpensive
magnifying glass nearby for
identifying pests.

045
OUTMANEUVER INSECTS

Occasionally the balance of predator and prey is thrown off balance, causing pest populations to grow. Unusually mild winters or rainy summers, for example, are common causes. If insect pest populations are on the rise, take a look at the damage to determine if pests are feeding directly on the harvestable parts of the plant. If so, they might warrant control. In most cases, if feeding on nonedible plant parts, these pests do not need control. When control is necessary, here are three methods to outmaneuver pests in your garden.

PHYSICAL

YOUR FINGERS Remove leaves that are heavily infested with insects or larvae. Handpick larger insects and toss infested foliage and insects into a bucket of soapy water; discard.

WATER Dislodge insects with a blast of water from a hose. Spray the entire plant, including the undersides of foliage. This works well for aphids, whiteflies, and spider mites. Repeat as often as needed.

BARRIERS Floating row covers keep flying insects from landing on plants to feed or lay eggs. Cardboard collars around seedlings prevent cutworms from reaching and chewing through stems.

TRAPS Commercial sticky traps attract insects such as leafhoppers and whiteflies. Many insect traps perform best as monitoring devices, alerting when pests arrive in the neighborhood; they are less effective at killing sufficient numbers to make a noticeable dent in pest populations.

BIOLOGICAL

Beneficial or predator insects carry out biological control by dining on pest insects. Some common beneficial creatures include assassin bugs, green lacewings, ladybugs, praying mantes, predatory mites, and spiders. Create a community of beneficial organisms in the soil by regularly mixing compost into the planting area. Avoid using pesticides, which kill beneficial insects along with the pests. And include predator-friendly plants in your garden. Herbs in the parsley family are among the most attractive plants to various beneficial insects. Plant several clusters in your garden.

CHEMICAL

Chemical controls are typically used as a last resort, after other control strategies have failed and the damage warrants intervention. There are many types of pest-control products, including organic options. No matter what type of chemical control you use, it is vital to select a target-specific product that acts against a limited number of species.

046 DO NO HARM
A chemical control product might eliminate a troublesome pest, but it might also harm beneficial insects like this monarch butterfly. Choose nonchemical control methods whenever possible.

047
BLAST AWAY

Banning the use of pesticides allows beneficial insects to deter pests. For instance, the Japanese lady beetle feeds on aphids. If you feel compelled to spray something on plants infested with aphids or other soft-bodied insect pests, reach for the garden hose instead and blast them with a forceful jet of water.

048
FIGHT OFF DISEASES

Diseases are caused by fungi, bacteria, or viruses. Fungi are minuscule organisms that live on plants, causing visible symptoms. Insects, water, and wind are typical ways they spread. Bacteria are single-cell organisms that live inside plants and are transferred from plant to plant by insects, water, and hands. Viruses are the smallest of the three and the most difficult to control. They are usually spread by insects, though some are spread by seeds and tools.

The best line of defense against diseases is prevention. Embrace these hygiene and prevention tips, and diseases will have trouble getting a toehold in your garden.

SELECT A SUITABLE SITE
Establish your garden in a sunny location with well-drained soil

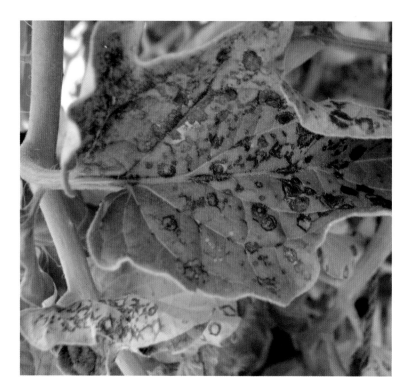

and good air circulation. Remove weeds from the garden and surrounding areas because they harbor many disease organisms.

PLANT RESISTANT VARIETIES
Whenever possible, choose varieties of plants bred to be resistant to debilitating diseases.

CULTIVATE DEEPLY
Whether by hand or with equipment, cultivate as deeply as possible to completely bury remnants of the previous crop or any disease organisms attached to them. Tilling to a depth of 10 to 12 inches (25–30 cm) is optimal.

CONTROL WEEDS
Certain weeds, particularly those related to the fruits and vegetables in your garden, may harbor viruses or other diseases that could move into your garden with the aid of insects that feed on both plants.

START DISEASE-FREE
Shop at a reputable nursery for healthy, disease-free transplants and certified disease-free seed potatoes.

ALWAYS ROTATE
The practice of rotating crops, or planting them in a different location every year, will help minimize pest problems. Many insects and diseases overwinter in the soil and spring forth the following year to attack plants in the same location. If their preferred host plants are not in the immediate vicinity, pests are less likely to reach problem status. Crop rotation is especially critical for members of the cabbage family and the tomato family, which should not be planted in the same space more than once every three years.

049
DECLARE WAR ON WEEDS

Weeds are divided into two categories. The first includes weeds that produce enormous quantities of seeds. These are often easy to kill, either with weed-control products or with a hoe, but new ones keep appearing. Weeds in the second category are hard to kill, often because they have persistent underground parts that can sprout into new plants. A few weeds, such as dandelions, have both of these characteristics.

Work to prevent weeds in early spring before the weeds get a strong foothold, and you'll nearly eliminate the weed war. Follow these prevention strategies.

MULCH A 2-inch (5-cm) layer of organic mulch, such as grass clippings or shredded bark, is an easy way to suppress weeds because mulch blocks light and prevents weed seed germination.

MULCH-FREE ZONE Prevent disease by maintaining a 2- to 3-inch (5–8-cm) mulch-free zone around the base of plants. Moist mulch in contact with stems, twigs, and trunks creates opportunity for fungi and bacteria to enter the plant.

PLANT COVER CROP Plant a small area with a cover crop,

such as wheat, barley, oats, rye, sorghum, or sudangrass. When the edible crop finishes its growing season, it will act as a mulch to shade the soil and prevent germination of weed seeds.

REMOVE ROOTS When removing weeds, remove as much root as possible. Use a small trowel or taproot weeder to pry pesky roots out of the ground. Regular weeding will keep weeds small and easy to pull and prevent weeds from setting seed and creating hundreds of new seedlings.

Test Garden Tip
050
AVOID TOXIC RESIDUES

Weed-control products are rarely used in food gardens. Toxicity to crops, difficulty in applying chemicals accurately, and the potential for toxic residues are the main reasons to avoid them.

CONTAINER GARDENING

Growing edibles in pots is convenient, attractive, and versatile for small spaces. Even if you plant the majority of your crop elsewhere on your landscape, container gardening lets you grow a few staples within arm's reach outside your door.

051
PLANT POTTED EDIBLES

No room for a garden? No problem! Follow these tips for a harvest of produce from a pot.

CONTAINERS The style of container isn't nearly as important as its size. Herbs, salad greens, green onions, and radishes prefer a container at least 4 inches (10 cm) deep; choose pots at least 8 inches (20 cm) deep for Swiss chard, peppers, eggplants, and baby carrots. Save large containers for tomatoes, broccoli, squash, and cucumbers. Make sure each pot has a drainage hole.

SOIL Garden soil is too dense for containers; use a commercial potting mix instead, and enrich it with compost and slow-release fertilizer mix (if it isn't already included). To reduce watering time, incorporate soil polymers into the potting mix. These compounds absorb moisture when wet and slowly release the water back into the potting mix as it dries out.

PLANTING Purchase seedlings of tomatoes, peppers, and eggplants, and transplant them one to a pot. Most other vegetables, including salad greens and bush cucumbers, can be grown from seeds sown directly in containers. For vegetables that are prone to sprawling, choose compact varieties. Asparagus, sweet corn, melons, and pumpkins are too big for containers.

SPACING Even in pots, vegetables don't like to be crowded. Follow the spacing recommendations on seed packets for carrots, beets, green onions, and radishes. For bush zucchini or cucumbers, sow several seeds in a pot; later, thin to leave only the strongest seedling. Salad greens are an exception to the no-crowding rule.

EXPOSURE Most vegetables and herbs need full days of sunlight—with a minimum of six hours of full sun per day. If your container vegetables are prone to wilting on the hottest summer days, give the plants some shade from midday to late in the afternoon. Leafy vegetables get by on at least four hours of full sun daily.

WATER Check pots daily and water early in the day to allow plants to soak up what they need before the afternoon heat. Watering in the evening can leave moisture on foliage and promote disease. If the top inch of soil feels dry, it's time to water. Spreading a 1-inch (2.5-cm) layer of mulch over the potting mix reduces moisture lost to evaporation.

Garden hoses and watering wands are popular choices, but there are other options. Using drip irrigation set on a timer delivers water near plant root zones with little evaporation and runoff. Self-watering pots feature built-in reservoirs that deliver moisture to the soil and require less frequent watering.

FERTILIZER Container vegetables need regular applications of fertilizer. Whether the potting mix included slow-release fertilizer or not, supplement with soluble all-purpose organic fertilizer throughout the growing season.

052
CHOOSE THE RIGHT CONTAINER

Size matters when it comes to the containers for edibles—if the pot is too small, your tomato plant might topple. If a fruit tree is planted in a massive container, you'll have a tough time lugging it inside at the end of the season. Use these sizes as a guide.

POT SIZE 1 gallon (4 L), 10-inch (25-cm) diameter and at least 6 inches (15 cm) deep
Herbs
Lettuce
Onion
Spinach

POT SIZE 4 to 5 gallons (15–19 L)
Beet
Carrot
Cucumber
Eggplant
Green Bean
Pepper
Potato
Tomato

POT SIZE 5 to 7 gallons (19–26 L)
Dwarf fruit trees

053
TRY AN EDIBLE PETAL

First taste a flower to find out how best to serve it; some flower petals are tasty, but their bases are tough. The whole flower might be edible, but that doesn't mean it's palatable. Remember to eat only organically grown flowers.

CHIVES The round heads of tiny lavender flowers are powerful in flavor; break them apart for salads. For more blooms, pick flowers before they go to seed. Both the blooms and thin, hollow leaves have a mild oniony flavor. A herbaceous perennial, chives die back in winter and return in spring. Plants spread to form clumps 12 inches (30 cm) tall and wide. They need full sun and well-drained soil.

NASTURTIUM The peppery flavor from both the leaves and flowers of this annual adds zip to sandwiches and salads. It's one of the easiest flowers to grow for a crop all season long. Some varieties, such as Dwarf Jewel Mix or variegated Alaska Mix, are more floriferous than climbers. Plants grow 12 inches (30 cm) tall and wide. They require full sun to partial shade and well-drained soil.

PANSY Pansies are annuals or half-hardy perennials that flower throughout the season and, in mild climates, in winter. From small-flower Johnny-jump-ups (V. tricolor) to large-flower hybrids, pansies are pretty in salads and on plates. Plants grow 12 inches (30 cm) tall and wide. They prefer full sun to partial shade and need well-drained soil.

DAYLILY Daylilies have a mild flavor and can be eaten raw or used in cooking, such as in a stir-fry. They also can be stuffed or used to make a beautiful little bowl. Many selections of this perennial are available, such as the dwarf long-blooming, yellow-flower 'Stella d'Oro.' Plants grow 3 feet (91 cm) tall and 1 foot (30 cm) wide. These flowers need full sun and well-drained soil.

CALENDULA Flowers flourish in spring and, in cool-weather regions, through summer. Use petals to color salads. Although calendula reseeds, get better flowering by using a fresh packet every year, starting indoors early. For continued flowering, deadhead constantly. Plants grow 24 inches (61 cm) tall and wide. They need full sun to partial shade and well-drained soil.

ROSE Two rugosa selections are preferred for culinary purposes: 'Hansa' and 'Buffalo Gal' (syn. 'Foxi'). Rose petals can be used fresh or dried. They can be tossed into a salad or used to flavor tea, honey, syrup, or ice cream. Plants grow 4 feet (1.2 m) tall and 3 feet (91 cm) wide. These flowers need full sun and well-drained soil.

PLANT AN ORCHARD

Don't be intimidated by the word orchard. Integrate the fruit trees into an existing shrub bed and they quickly become landscape plants. Whether you choose to grow two fruit trees or a half-acre orchard, here are a few particulars to keep in mind.

Test Garden Tip

054
GET SMALL

Even the smallest yard usually has space for a fruit tree. For years, scientists have been working to select and produce small, productive fruit trees for home landscapes. When shopping at the nursery, check the plant tag for important information about tree height and spread.

055
ORGANIZE YOUR ORCHARD

Before you start digging holes around your property and ordering fruit trees from those beautiful catalogs, spend some time planning. You won't regret it.

SITE SPECIFICS Selecting a site for a fruit tree involves taking stock of the planting site's current conditions and predicting future conditions. Fruit trees require full sun for good growth and fruit production, so pay close attention to nearby trees, which may cast shade on the young fruit tree in 5 or 10 years as the plants mature. Fertile, well-drained soil is essential. Like most edibles, fruit trees will grow poorly, if at all, in heavy clay soil.

ENSURE POLLINATION Several types of fruit require more than one variety for pollination and subsequent fruit production. These plants set fruit only when they receive pollen from a nearby plant of a different variety. These types of plants are called self-sterile and include some peaches, apricots, crabapples, most apples, pears, plums, and sweet cherries. 'Royal Ann' sweet cherry, for example, must be within 100 feet (30 m) of another cherry tree with compatible pollen that blooms at the same time or it will not produce any cherries.

CARE AND MAINTENANCE When given regular care, fruit trees will produce bushels of fruit 3 to 5 years after planting. Deep watering is essential during the first year after planting. To encourage strong root growth, soak the tree root zone every week or two during the first year after planting. Drought conditions will require more frequent watering. Prevent competition for moisture by removing weeds and grass from underneath the tree canopy. Spread a 4- to 6-inch (10–15-cm) layer of mulch under the tree, keeping it away from the trunk. Plan to prune fruit trees every two to three years to ensure strong branching structure that will support developing fruit.

056
MIX IT UP
Plant care and pollination
are often simplified when
several different fruit trees are
planted together in a small
backyard orchard.

ALL ABOUT PRUNING

A few simple pruning practices will ensure your fruiting trees and shrubs produce bushels of fruit year after year. Snipping back healthy canes and pruning branches are important parts of maintaining a productive fruit planting. These step-by-step tips take the guesswork out of pruning.

057
PREVENT PROBLEMS WITH PRUNING

Just as thinning crowded seedlings is part of growing healthy vegetables, pruning and training is part of growing healthy fruit crops.

Don't be overwhelmed by pruning. A backyard fruit tree or shrub planting is a cinch to prune in 60 minutes or less on a crisp winter day.

WHY PRUNE?

Think of pruning as preventive maintenance. Trees and shrubs will live, grow, and bear fruit without ever being pruned, but experience has shown that good pruning and some training can prevent or remedy many of the problems that arise in growing fruit.

Removing branches allows sunlight to filter into the tree canopy, which will promote uniform ripening, increase the fruits' sugar content, and decrease disease problems because fruit and foliage will dry quickly after rainfall. Pruning shrubs has similar benefits.

WHAT TO PRUNE

TREES All fruit trees benefit from pruning. Dwarf fruit trees naturally retain their short stature, yet annual pruning will ensure that light can easily reach the center of the tree. Occasional pruning at the top of the tree will limit its height. When to prune fruit trees depends on type of tree and climate. In general, fruit trees are pruned in the dormant season.

BRAMBLES Raspberries and other cane fruits produce berries on one- and two-year-old canes. When the canes finish fruiting, they die back to the ground. Pruning removes these unnecessary canes and thins any spindly new growth to promote big berries and healthy plants. Brambles are often pruned during the dormant season or after fruiting.

SHRUBS Pruning a shrub involves thinning the bush by trimming off stems at ground level. Dense, twiggy growth prevents sunlight from reaching the center of the plant, which limits fruit production.

GRAPES Extensive pruning and training is required to produce top-quality grape clusters. Prune after leaves fall off in autumn and before new growth emerges in spring.

058
MAKE THE CUT ON FRUIT TREES

The two basic types of pruning cuts are heading and thinning cuts. Heading is the process of shortening a branch, not removing it entirely, and encourages buds on the remaining portion of the branch to sprout new growth.

When fruits are about the size of a quarter, select the largest and remove nearby fruits so there is a distance of twice the expected diameter of the mature fruit between all remaining fruits.

When pruning limbs and small branches, make a pruning cut just beyond where the offending limb attaches to the larger branch or tree. This area is called the branch collar; it contains tissue that prevents decay. If disease does make its way into the branch through the wound, the chemicals in the branch collar will prevent it from infecting the rest of the tree.

When pruning branches more than 1½ inches (4 cm) in diameter, use a three-part cut. The first is an undercut from the bottom of the branch about 6 to 12 inches (15–30 cm) out from the trunk and about one third of the way through the branch. Make a second cut about 3 inches (8 cm) beyond the undercut, cutting until the branch falls away. Cut the resulting stub back to the branch collar. Always make cuts close to a node (point of leaf attachment or branching) and at a slight angle to reduce pests and disease.

059 KNOW YOUR TOOLS

Good pruning equipment ensures smooth cuts that are less likely to be invaded by insects. When you have these tools on hand, pruning will be a breeze.

HAND PRUNERS You'll use these more often than any other tool. Invest in a high-quality, ergonomically designed pair.

FOLDING PRUNING SAW Small enough to tote around with ease but sharp enough to make quick work of cutting off limbs, a folding pruning saw is essential.

LONG-HANDLE LOPPERS Thanks to the leverage provided by long-handled loppers, you can easily cut through 1-inch- (2.5-cm-) thick branches. They also are indispensable for reaching into thorny brambles and dense shrubs.

POLE PRUNERS Reach the top of a dwarf fruit tree from ground level with pole pruners. The handle can extend 10 to 15 feet (3–4.6 m).

CHAPTER 2

Spring

PEAS

Forget the mushy canned peas you grew up with; freshly picked peas will add a sweet crunch to any meal. These frost-hardy vegetables are high in protein, iron, and fiber and can be grown almost anywhere that's sunny. Peas taste like spring, a little sweet and a little grassy.

Green, succulent, and sweet, garden peas intended for cooking and eating fresh weren't developed until the 1500s. Since then many varieties of fresh peas have appeared, including three of the most common in American gardens—sugar peas, snow peas, and shelling peas. Both sugar peas (sometimes called sugar snap peas) and snow peas have tender, stringless edible pods, but the pods of sugar peas are fleshier, sweeter, and remain tasty and tender as the seeds inside mature. The whole pod of a sugar pea is a sweet, crunchy treat, one of the kid-friendliest vegetables. Snow peas and the tender tips of their vines are frequent ingredients in stir-fry recipes. That flavorful Asian connection is probably because snow peas adapt better to warm-climate gardens than do sugar and shelling peas. Gardeners can grow big meaty green peas (the shelling peas common to school lunch trays) as well as the delicate petit pois of French cuisine. Whatever you have in mind, all peas grow in similar conditions, so there is no need to choose just one variety.

060
PLANT, GROW & HARVEST

SITE Plant peas in a location where they can be protected from midday sun when temperatures are higher than 80°F (27°C). Peas do best in rich, well-drained soil.

BEDMATES Interplant peas with corn, tomatoes, garlic, and lettuce.

CARE Peas can be damaged by a late frost, and tolerate brief periods of temperatures to 25°F (−4°C), but prolonged exposure will interfere with development. Flowers drop and vines wither in temperatures warmer than 80°F (27°C). All but the most dwarf plants require supports for the vines to climb.

HOW TO START Grow from seeds.

HARVEST Pick snap varieties when pods are plump and seeds are fully developed. Harvest snow peas when pods are flat and seeds are small and undeveloped. Shelling or English peas are ready to pick when pods are fully rounded.

PESTS AND DISEASES Peas may be susceptible to leaf spot, blights and rusts, fusarium wilt, powdery mildew, botrytis and other molds, damping off, and mosaic virus. Choose varieties bred for resistance to bacteria and fungi, and rotate crops each year. Beneficial insects control most aphids and thrips. Use insecticidal soap spray if infestations are severe, and set up floating row covers on young plants to discourage weevils.

061 TAKE THESE TIPS TO THE GARDEN

SOW SEEDS When the soil temperature is at least 45°F (7°C), plant seeds 1 to 1½ inches (2.5–4 cm) deep with 1 inch (3 cm) between seeds (A).

PLANT PEAS For easy harvesting, the rows should be 18 to 24 inches (46–61 cm) apart (B).

SUPPORT PLANTS Most varieties are self-supporting. For those that aren't, help train tendrils onto a fence or other support (C).

HARVEST It's time to pick shelling peas when the pods are swollen and start to feel plump (D).

The sugar content in peas begins to decline as soon as the peas are harvested. To eat them at their sweetest, pick them right before cooking — or freeze them within three hours of harvest.

062 KNOW YOUR VARIETIES

SHELLING PEAS

Green peas, also called English peas, are cultivars grown for shelling:

'DAKOTA' This early variety is ready to harvest in 50 to 55 days.

'CASELOAD' An extra-sweet shelling pea, ready in 55 to 60 days.

'MAESTRO' AND 'ECLIPSE' Both of these varieties are good choices for hot climates.

SNOW PEAS

PISUM SATIVUM VAR. MACROCARPON These varieties are grown for their edible pods, called snow peas, which may require stringing.

'OREGON GIANT' This disease-resistant variety produces sweet large pods in 60 to 70 days and throughout the summer.

'SUGAR POD2' Best for cool climates, bearing in 60 to 70 days.

SUGAR PEAS

Other edible-pod varieties, called snap peas, are harvested after the seeds have filled out.

'SUGAR ANN' This variety is the earliest to harvest. It's ready in just 50 to 55 days.

'SUGAR SNAP' Boasting plump, succulent pods, this variety is ready to harvest in 60 to 70 days in both cool and hot weather.

'SUPER SUGAR SNAP' This is a powdery mildew–resistant variety.

063
TOSS A LITTLE TARRAGON INTO YOUR PEAS

Two types of peas—one shelled and one in the pod—are flavored with butter, lemon zest, cracked pepper, and tarragon. Tarragon has an assertive licoricey flavor. If you're not a fan, substitute fresh basil.

PREP: 15 minutes   COOK: 12 minutes   MAKES: 6 servings

½   cup (125 mL) water

3½   cups (525 g) shelled fresh English peas

1½   cups (95 g) whole fresh sugar snap pea pods and/or snow pea pods

1   tablespoon butter, softened

1   tablespoon snipped fresh tarragon

2   teaspoons lemon zest

½   teaspoon freshly cracked black pepper

¼   teaspoon salt

STEP 1 In a medium saucepan bring the water to boiling. Add shelled English peas. Return to boiling; reduce heat. Simmer, covered, for 8 minutes. Add the whole sugar snap peas. Cook, covered, for 4 minutes or just until crisp-tender; drain.

STEP 2 Add butter, tarragon, lemon zest black pepper, and salt to the peas. Toss gently until butter is melted. Serve immediately.

EACH SERVING *91 cal, 2 g fat, 4 mg chol, 19 mg sodium, 14 g carb, 5 g fiber, 5 g pro*

064
SMASH YOUR PEAS

These toasts—spread with ricotta and the creamy blend of mashed peas and edamame, flavored with garlic, mint, lemon juice, and pepper—make a nice appetizer or side dish.

START TO FINISH: 30 minutes   MAKES: 8 servings

1	16-ounce (450-g) package frozen baby sweet peas
1	12-ounce (340-g) package frozen sweet soybeans (edamame), shelled
1	tablespoon olive oil
4	cloves garlic, sliced
¼	cup (5 g) snipped fresh mint
2	tablespoons lemon juice
1	to 2 teaspoons freshly ground black pepper
½	teaspoon kosher salt
½	1-pound (450 g) baguette, sliced and toasted
1	cup (246 g) ricotta cheese
	Kosher salt and freshly ground black pepper
	Extra-virgin olive oil (optional)

STEP 1 In large pot cook peas and soybeans in a small amount of boiling water for 5 minutes or until tender. Drain in a colander. Transfer peas and edamame to a food processor; cover and process until almost smooth. Transfer pureed mixture to a serving bowl.

STEP 2 In a small skillet heat oil over medium heat. Add garlic; cook 1 to 2 minutes or until tender. Add garlic, mint, lemon juice, pepper, and salt to pureed pea mixture.

STEP 3 For ricotta toasts, spread toasted baguette slices with the ricotta cheese. Arrange on baking sheet. Broil about 4 inches (10 cm) from heat for 1 to 2 minutes or until ricotta is warm. Sprinkle with salt and pepper.

STEP 4 If desired, drizzle peas with olive oil and sprinkle with additional black pepper. Serve with ricotta toasts.

EACH SERVING *274 cal, 11 g fat, 16 mg chol, 458 mg sodium, 30 g carb, 6 g fiber, 15 g pro*

LETTUCES & GREENS

Fill your garden with a blend of lettuce for colorful meals. Looseleaf, butterhead (sometimes called Boston lettuce), and romaine (or cos) are three common lettuce varieties. Include other greens, such as arugula, mâche, cress, mustard, chicory, and mizuna, to create tasty salads. Crisp leaf lettuce, succulent head varieties, spicy mesclun, dark-green spinach—there are so many types and tastes of greens.

Greens aren't all green. Swiss chard offers rainbow red, yellow, and white stems. Radicchio features red leaves. Many lettuces have spots and splashes of color that make them beautiful in a big bowl. Texture is another feature. Curly and flat-leaf varieties make for a varied salad too.

Lettuce greens are a health food—most varieties of lettuce, especially dark green- and red-leafed, are high in vitamins A and C, folate, and nutrients. It's fast too. Growing lettuce from seed packet to table takes only about a month. As temperatures climb into summer, spring lettuce plants begin to set seed, which causes leaves to become bitter and inedible. This process, bolting, occurs as night temperatures remain about 70°F (21°C). When plants begin to bolt, pull them up and compost them. Swiss chard is a green that grows all summer without bolting. Minimize weeds by planting lettuce tightly, with leaves of individual plants touching.

065
PLANT, GROW & HARVEST

SITE Choose a site with full sun to partial shade and loose, fertile soil.

BEDMATES Plant lettuce around taller plants such as broccoli or peppers.

CARE As seedlings grow, thin plants to 4 to 6 inches (10–15 cm) apart. Eat young plants as you thin them.

HOW TO START Start head lettuce indoors 6 weeks before the last frost date and transplant outdoors 3 weeks before the last frost date. Direct-sow other lettuces in early spring or fall.

HARVEST Cut head lettuce about 1 inch (2.5 cm) above the lowest leaves. Snap individual leaves from the outer edges of loose-leaf lettuces as soon as plants are big enough to spare a few leaves. Cut baby lettuce leaf blends or mesclun with scissors about 1 inch (2.5 cm) above the lowest leaves.

PESTS AND DISEASES To discourage cutworms, use a paper collar around young lettuce seedlings. Repel slugs with a sprinkling of wood ashes or diatomaceous earth on the soil around plants; reapply after each rainfall. Look for aphids on the underside of tender leaves or hidden inside the crown of plants. Use insecticidal soap to control pests. To prevent fungal and bacterial diseases, rotate lettuce crops each year.

066 TAKE THESE TIPS TO THE GARDEN

SOW SEEDS Plant seeds directly into the ground or plant sprouts. Water seeds and sprouts lightly to keep soil moist and cool but not wet (A).

GROW LETTUCE Decorative pots are an attractive choice for growing lettuce when space is limited. Three or four 18-inch (46-cm) pots will hold enough for a spring season of salads. Lettuces are so shallow rooted that they will also grow in window boxes (B).

USE A COLD FRAME This protective frame is used to grow lettuces in cold weather—early spring and late fall (C).

orange stalks. Leaves are eaten raw when young; mature leaves can be cooked or sautéed, which takes away the slightly bitter taste.

ARUGULA OR ROCKET Native to the Mediterranean region, when harvested young, this leafy green adds peppery flavor to salads. Mature leaves can be sautéed.

CHERVIL This delicate herb has close family ties to parsley. Its anise flavor and fernlike leaves add spice to salads.

CLAYTONIA This salad green is nicknamed miner's lettuce for the California gold rush miners who ate the vitamin C–rich leaves to prevent scurvy. The succulent leaves resemble tiny lily pads.

CORN SALAD This lettuce is also called mâche and lamb's lettuce, and it grows wild in parts of Europe, North Africa, and Asia. Its pretty rosettes of soft, delicate leaves have a mild, nutty flavor.

CURLY ENDIVE Also known as chicory or frisée, curly endive adds a pleasantly bitter flavor and texture to salads. The finely cut leaves contrast with smooth, succulent leaves of Belgian endive, which are often used as crunchy bases for hors d'oeuvres.

GARDEN CRESS This land-loving relative of watercress has a peppery flavor. Leaves are used as garnishes or added to salads, sandwiches, and soups.

KALE The curly leaves of kale—a loose-head form of cabbage—sweeten in cold temperatures. Colorful, ornamental varieties are also edible.

067
KNOW YOUR VARIETIES

MESCLUN Often sold as field or baby greens, mesclun is a mix of young greens such as lettuces, endive, arugula, mizuna, chard, radicchio, and mustard greens.

RADICCHIO OR RED CHICORY This plant produces compact round cabbagelike heads of deep red leaves that have a slightly bitter taste. Individual leaves are often used as garnish.

MIZUNA One of many types of mustard greens, mizuna is a member of the Brassica family. Its ornamental leaves are sweeter than its cabbage and kale relatives.

PAK CHOI This Chinese cabbage (often spelled bok choy) forms ornamental vase-shape heads. The green leaves and white stems are sweet and crunchy, fresh or stir-fried.

SWISS CHARD A highly ornamental green with large leaves and contrasting ribbed veins. Varieties have red, yellow, or

068
GO GREEN WITH LETTUCE & PEAS

This salad of butter lettuce, peas, and slivered endive dressed with a mustard vinaigrette celebrates the colors of spring. The sweetness of the peas and the pleasant bitterness of the endive balance each other perfectly.

START TO FINISH: 30 minutes   MAKES: 6 servings

2	cups (300 g) shelled fresh peas or frozen peas
1	tablespoon snipped fresh dill
1	tablespoon lemon juice
1	tablespoon cider vinegar
2	teaspoons Dijon-style mustard
¼	teaspoon salt
¼	teaspoon freshly ground black pepper
3	tablespoons olive oil
2	small heads Belgian endive
1	large head butter or Bibb lettuce, separated into leaves
	Freshly ground black pepper
3	tablespoons chopped macadamia nuts, toasted (optional)
	Chive blossom florets* or snipped fresh chives (optional)

STEP 1 Fill a medium saucepan with water. Bring to boiling over high heat. Add peas; cook for 1 minute, stirring once. Immediately drain in a colander. Rinse with cold water. Drain peas again and set aside.

STEP 2 For mustard vinaigrette, in a medium bowl combine dill, lemon juice, vinegar, mustard, salt, and the ¼ teaspoon pepper. Slowly add the oil in a thin stream, whisking until fully blended. Add peas to vinaigrette; toss to coat.

STEP 3 Slice endive in half lengthwise and remove core, then slice lengthwise into thin strips. Add to the pea mixture; lightly toss to combine.

STEP 4 Arrange lettuce on a platter; top with pea mixture. Sprinkle with additional pepper. If desired, top with nuts and chive blossom florets.

*TIP Break the chive blossom from the stem to get florets.

EACH SERVING *107 cal, 7 g fat, 0 mg chol, 142 mg sodium, 8 g carb, 3 g fiber, 3 g pro*

069
WHIP UP A CITRUS SALAD

Tender Bibb lettuce and juicy segments of pink grapefruit and clementines get tossed with an orange-tarragon-mustard vinaigrette and topped with toasted coconut in this most refreshing salad.

START TO FINISH: 20 minutes   **MAKES:** 6 servings

3	oranges
¼	cup (50 mL) extra-virgin olive oil
1	tablespoon snipped fresh tarragon
1	tablespoon Dijon-style mustard
2	heads Bibb lettuce, torn
1	pink grapefruit, peeled and thinly sliced
2	clementines, peeled and separated into segments
½	cup (37.5 g) unsweetened flaked coconut, toasted*

STEP 1 For dressing, squeeze juice from 1 orange and transfer to a small bowl. Whisk in oil, tarragon, and mustard.

STEP 2 Peel and thinly slice the remaining 2 oranges.

STEP 3 Place lettuce in a large bowl. Drizzle with dressing; toss to coat. Add orange slices, grapefruit slices, and clementine segments. Lightly toss to mix. Arrange salad on platter. Sprinkle with toasted coconut.

*TIP To toast coconut, preheat oven to 350°F (175°C). Spread coconut in a shallow baking pan. Bake 5 to 8 minutes or until lightly browned, shaking pan once or twice and watching carefully to prevent burning.

EACH SERVING *211 cal, 15 g fat, 0 mg chol, 67 mg sodium, 19 g carb, 5 g fiber, 3 g pro*

CARROTS & RADISHES

Long and slender or golf-ball round, orange, red, white, purple, or yellow—carrots come in so many fun sizes and colors. Sure, you can grow traditional large orange carrots, but you can also have fun with the many sizes and colors available to grow from seed.

Carrots are loaded with vitamin A and beta-carotene, both known as antioxidants and cancer fighters. Cooking carrots makes the calcium in them more available, which is another nutritional bonus.

Radishes are early gratification for gardeners. Few vegetables grow as quickly and easily as radishes. In less than a month after planting seeds, these crunchy, peppery roots are ready to serve in salads. Growing radishes with kids is fun because radishes germinate quickly and they are so easy to harvest; plucking these little gems from the earth is a treat.

Small radishes are ready to harvest in as little as three weeks from sowing. Large radishes, daikon, or winter radishes require longer—between 50 and 55 days to mature. Because radishes germinate and grow so quickly, they are ideal to interplant with slow-to-emerge carrots. Radish seedlings actually help carrots grow better because they break the soil crust for the slower-growing root crop. By the time interplanted carrots need more space, radishes are ready to be harvested.

070
PLANT, GROW & HARVEST

SITE Choose a sunny location with loose, fertile soil. Rake the soil free of rocks.

BEDMATES Sow radish seeds together with carrots. Both are early-season crops, but radishes will be ready for harvest first, leaving room for carrots to develop fully without the need for thinning. Interplant carrots and radishes with lettuces, beans, peas, tomatoes, and peppers.

CARE When radish and carrot seedlings are about 2 inches (5 cm) tall, thin the plants.

HOW TO START Grow carrots and radishes from seeds. Sow in early spring, 2 to 4 weeks before the last frost date. Wet the soil before planting to prevent seeds from blowing away. Sow carrot seeds in raised rows 12 inches (31 cm) apart. Cover seeds with ¼ inch (6 mm) of fine soil. Keep soil lightly moist—use a mister to water to avoid washing away seeds.

HARVEST Begin pulling carrots as soon as they develop full color to allow the remaining carrots to grow larger without becoming misshapen. For winter storage, wait to harvest until after the tops have been exposed to several frosts; cold will increase their sweetness.

PESTS AND DISEASES Crop rotation solves most disease problems for carrots and radishes, and they are virtually disease- and pest-free.

071 TAKE THESE TIPS TO THE GARDEN

RADISHES Begin harvesting radishes when they are less than 1 inch (2.5 cm) in diameter, pulling them to eat until they become spongy or cracked. Plant in spring and again in autumn (A).

CARROTS Harvest carrots when they reach the full color for the variety (B).

CARROTS Keep harvesting carrots as the weather cools. Keep them in the ground, cutting back foliage (C), and mulch heavily with straw (D). Dig them throughout winter or in early spring before new growth starts.

073
KNOW YOUR RADISH VARIETIES

'CHERRIETTE' This variety grows well either as a spring or a fall crop, and is ready to harvest 26 days from planting.

'D'AVIGNON' A traditional variety from the south of France, the elongated red radishes with a white tip are ready in just 21 days.

'FRENCH BREAKFAST' bears white-tipped scarlet roots that have a sweet, mild flavor. Roots are ready in 23 to 28 days.

'MINOWASE SUMMER CROSS NO. 3' DAIKON RADISH Best as a fall crop, it produces 8- to 10-inch- (20–25-cm-) long tapered white roots in 55 days from seeding.

'NERO TONDO' A winter radish featuring round black roots with crisp white flesh. The 2- to 4-inch-diameter (5 to 10 cm) roots take 50 days to mature.

'WHITE ICICLE' produces 4- to 5-inch (10–12 cm) tapered white roots. Despite their large size, they have mild flavor. 35 days.

072
KNOW YOUR CARROT VARIETIES

'DANVERS 126' This is a heat-resistant variety with tapered, thin, 7-inch- (18-cm-) long roots. It is ready to harvest in 75 days.

'IMPERATOR 58' This variety bears sweet, tender roots in 70 days. It grows best in loose soils to about 9 inches (23 cm) long.

'KURODA' This variety produces large yields in 70 days. It grows up to 12 inches (31 cm) long in sandy soils. It has an orange core and its color fades with cooking.

'RED-CORED CHANTENAY' This heirloom carrot variety has a deep orange color from skin to core and wide shoulders that taper to a point. It is ready to harvest within 65 days.

'THUMBELINA' This small, round carrot is good for growing in heavy soils and ready to pick in 60 days. It grows to 2-inches- (5-cm-) long and is good for baking or roasting.

074
ROAST YOUR RADISHES

Peppery radishes mellow when roasted and their characteristic crisp texture turns tender. Lightly dressed in a chive vinaigrette, they make a tasty side dish for roast chicken.

PREP: 15 minutes   **ROAST:** 30 minutes at 425°F (220°C)   **MAKES:** 6 servings

1½	pounds (700 g) radishes, trimmed, scrubbed, and halved
3	tablespoons olive oil
2	tablespoons white wine vinegar
1	tablespoon snipped fresh chives
½	teaspoon Dijon-style mustard
¼	teaspoon black pepper
⅛	teaspoon salt

STEP 1 Preheat oven to 425°F (220°C). In a medium bowl toss radishes with 1 tablespoon of the oil. Place the radishes in a 15×10×1-inch (40×25×2-cm) baking pan. Roast, uncovered, for 30 to 35 minutes or until tender and lightly browned, stirring once.

STEP 2 For chive vinaigrette, in a screw-top jar combine the remaining 2 tablespoons oil, the vinegar, chives, mustard, pepper, and salt. Drizzle vinaigrette over radishes; toss to coat.

EACH SERVING *80 cal, 7 g fat, 0 mg chol, 103 mg sodium, 4 g carb, 2 g fiber, 1 g pro*

075
BRAISE YOUR CARROTS

This spring medley of carrots, mushrooms, pearl onions, and asparagus is flash-braised in white wine. If you can get your hands on morel mushrooms, their meaty texture and delicate flavor is worth the price.

START TO FINISH: 25 minutes   MAKES: 6 servings

2	tablespoons butter
1½	pounds (700 g) young spring carrots, trimmed and scrubbed, or large carrots, peeled and cut into 3-inch (8-cm) pieces
8	ounces (225 g) button mushrooms, quartered, and/or other mushrooms, such as oyster or morel*
6	ounces (170 g) pearl or whole boiling onions, peeled
3	cloves garlic, chopped
½	cup (125 mL) dry white wine or chicken broth
1	cup (250 mL) chicken broth
2	tablespoons snipped fresh marjoram
½	teaspoon kosher salt
¼	teaspoon freshly ground black pepper
8	ounces (225 g) fresh asparagus, trimmed and cut into 2- to 3-inch (5- to 8-cm) pieces
	Lemon wedges (optional)

STEP 1 In an extra-large skillet melt butter over medium heat. Add carrots and mushrooms; cook for 3 minutes, stirring occasionally. Add onions and garlic; cook and stir for 2 minutes more. Increase heat to medium-high. Carefully add wine; cook for 1 minute or until wine has almost evaporated. Add broth, 1 tablespoon of the marjoram, the salt, and pepper; reduce heat to medium.

STEP 2 Cover; cook 8 to 10 minutes or until vegetables are fork-tender. Remove from heat. Add asparagus; cover. Let stand for 5 minutes. Sprinkle with the remaining marjoram. Serve with lemon wedges if desired.

*TIP If using morel mushrooms, place them in a bowl. Cover with water; add a dash of salt. Soak mushrooms 10 to 15 minutes. Drain, rinse, and repeat twice. Pat mushrooms dry. Trim ends of stems, if necessary, before adding to other vegetables in the skillet.

EACH SERVING *132 cal, 4 g fat, 11 mg chol, 425 mg sodium, 19 g carb, 5 g fiber, 4 g pro*

ASPARAGUS

It's hard to beat the sweet, nutty flavor of just-picked asparagus. Asparagus (*Asparagus officinalis*) has been grown for thousands of years—growing wild in fields, it's a spring treat for foragers. Grown in the garden, it's a reliable crop that produces juicy spears. Asparagus comes in green and purple varieties. White asparagus is simply asparagus grown without light.

Properly planted and tended asparagus beds produce tender, tasty spears every spring—for decades. One of the few perennial vegetables in American gardens, asparagus grows well in regions that have cold winter temperatures, which allow the plants to go dormant for a few weeks.

In ideal situations asparagus grows fast—up to 10 inches (25 cm) a day—so harvest often as soon as spears begin to show. The first season that you plant, allow asparagus to grow without harvesting. The following spring, harvest spears that are ½ inch (12 mm) in diameter. To help plants become established, harvest only for about two weeks.

Each crown produces spears for 6 to 7 weeks during the spring and early summer. Pick asparagus every 4 to 5 days; as weather warms, you may be able to harvest spears every day. Then allow the shoots to develop into tall, ferny growth—up to 6 feet (1.8 m) tall—to allow them to build a strong root system to pump out more asparagus the following year.

076
PLANT, GROW & HARVEST

SITE Choose a sunny location with light, fertile, and well-drained soil. Plan for future space needs because mature crowns may grow up to 24 inches (61 cm) wide.

BEDMATES Plant asparagus where it has not grown before.

CARE Asparagus does well in soil pH slightly higher than 7.0. Control weeds in the bed and dress the asparagus rows each autumn or early spring with compost. In spring, apply a balanced fertilizer (10-10-10, 12-12-12, etc.). Water frequently until plants are established and continue to water during hot weather. Cut back foliage after plants have gone dormant.

HOW TO START When you transplant year-old dormant roots, called crowns, you can harvest one year sooner than planting younger crowns or seeds.

HARVEST Gather asparagus in spring as stalks emerge, using a paring knife to cut just below the soil surface. Check daily because stalks grow fast. Continue harvesting until stalks look spindly.

PESTS AND DISEASES The fungus fusarium can rot stems and crowns. Disinfect seeds and roots with fungicide before planting. Control asparagus rust with a fungicide and asparagus beetles and aphids with specifically labeled pesticides.

077 TAKE THESE TIPS TO THE GARDEN

PLANT Asparagus does best in deep, rich, well-drained soil with a neutral pH. Dig a trench 1 foot (30 cm) or so wide and deep. Space rows about 4 feet (1.2 m) apart (A).

SPREAD Place root crowns 18 to 24 inches (46–61 cm) apart on shallow mounds of enriched soil in the trench (B).

COVER Use 2 inches (5 cm) of soil to cover crowns and water well (C). As shoots appear, add 2 inches (5 cm) of soil until the bed is level with the surrounding garden.

HARVEST Cut spears when they're at least 5 inches (13 cm) tall and ½ inch (12 mm) in diameter (D). Look for closed tips.

078
KNOW YOUR VARIETIES

'JERSEY GIANT' is the most widely grown variety, and it's more disease-resistant and productive than older varieties. Green spears with purplish tips are all male, so no energy is spent on flowering and seed production.

'UC 157' is the optimal choice for warm-winter regions. Developed in California, it's better suited to hot, dry conditions.

'PURPLE PASSION' bears purple spears that are sweeter than green ones, but yield is less. Spears turn green when cooked.

After harvest season, the lacy green asparagus foliage will grow 4 to 6 feet (1.2–1.8 m) tall. Keep plants watered, weeded, and mulched all summer. Cut back stems to 2-inch (5-cm) stubs in late fall.

079
STIR UP SOME ASPARAGUS SOUP

Grilling asparagus before cooking and pureeing gives the finished soup a lovely smoky flavor that's accented by spicy chili croutons.

PREP: 10 minutes GRILL: 4 minutes COOK: 15 minutes MAKES: 4 servings

4	tablespoons butter, melted
1½	to 2 tablespoons sriracha
1	small baguette, sliced diagonally
2	pounds (1 kg) green, white, and/or purple asparagus, trimmed
2	tablespoons butter
⅓	cup (50 g) finely chopped onion
¼	teaspoon salt
3	tablespoons all-purpose flour
½	teaspoon ground coriander
2	14.5-ounce (411-g) cans reduced-sodium chicken broth
½	cup (125 mL) milk
1	tablespoon lemon juice
	Olive oil (optional)

STEP 1 For chili croutons, in a bowl stir together the melted butter and sriracha; brush one side of each baguette slice with some of the mixture. Grill over medium heat 2 minutes or until toasted, turning once.

STEP 2 Add asparagus to remaining mixture. Grill over medium heat 2 to 4 minutes or until crisp-tender, turning once. Set aside one-fourth of the spears. Slice the remaining spears in ½-inch (1.2-cm) pieces.

STEP 3 In a saucepan melt the 2 tablespoons butter over medium heat. Cook onion 5 minutes or until tender. Add salt. Sprinkle flour over onions; cook and stir 1 minute. Stir in the coriander. Slowly whisk in broth. Add sliced asparagus. Simmer, uncovered, 10 minutes or until thickened.

STEP 4 Transfer soup to a food processor or blender, in batches if necessary. Cover and process or blend until smooth. Return soup to saucepan. Stir in milk and heat through. Add lemon juice. Cut the reserved asparagus spears into 2-inch (5-cm) lengths; add to soup. If desired, drizzle servings with olive oil. Serve with chili croutons.

EACH SERVING *310 cal, 13 g fat, 33 mg chol, 1029 mg sodium, 38 g carb, 4 g fiber, 11 g pro*

080
SANDWICH YOUR SPEARS

Asparagus, prosciutto, arugula, and provolone provide the filling for these toasty panini. If you don't have a panini press, simply grill them in a skillet; weight the sandwiches with a second skillet and a few heavy cans.

PREP: 25 minutes   COOK: 5 minutes   MAKES: 4 servings

16 asparagus spears, approximately 12 ounces (340 g)

8   very thin prosciutto slices, approximately 5 ounces (142 g)

8   slices rustic Italian bread

1   tablespoon coarse ground mustard

1   cup (21 g) lightly packed arugula (optional)

8   thin slices provolone cheese

1   tablespoon balsamic vinaigrette

STEP 1 Snap off and discard woody bases from asparagus. Trim stalks barely longer than bread slices. Place a steamer rack in the bottom of a large saucepan and add water to just below the basket. Bring to boiling. Add asparagus. Cover and reduce heat. Steam 3 to 5 minutes or until crisp-tender. Transfer to a bowl of ice water for 30 seconds to cool; drain.

STEP 2 Cut prosciutto in half lengthwise. For each spear of asparagus, starting at the base, wrap 1 halved prosciutto piece diagonally to the top of the spear.

STEP 3 Spread 4 slices of bread with mustard. Place 4 prosciutto-wrapped spears horizontally on each mustard-topped bread slice. If desired, top with arugula. Add 2 slices of cheese to each sandwich to completely cover bread. Lightly brush remaining 4 bread slices with balsamic vinaigrette. Place bread, vinaigrette sides down, on top of cheese.

STEP 4 Preheat a panini press; place sandwiches (half at a time, if necessary) in grill. Cover and cook 4 to 5 minutes or until cheese is melted. (Or place sandwiches in preheated grill pan or skillet. Weight sandwiches with another skillet with cans of food as added weight. Grill 3 minutes or until bread is toasted. Turn sandwiches, weight, and grill until toasted, 2 to 3 minutes).

EACH SERVING *402 cal, 15 g fat, 54 mg chol, 1713 mg sodium, 39 g carb, 4 g fiber, 29 g pro*

BROCCOLI & CAULIFLOWER

With similar growth habits and flavors, broccoli and cauliflower are members of the vegetable genus *Brassica*, which includes Brussels sprouts, cabbage, collard greens, kale, and kohlrabi.

Cauliflower is related to wild cabbage and grows similarly to broccoli. Cauliflower (*Brassica oleracea* Botrytis Group) has a thick stem with a series of tight flower buds at the top, which is called a curd. Cauliflower has large leaves that shade the curd to remain white. This protection is called blanching and keeps the area white because shade affects the production of chlorophyll. However, there are varieties of nonwhite cauliflowers. Orange, lime green, or purple cauliflowers present beautiful serving possibilities for raw vegetable platters.

There are two types of broccoli. Sprouting broccoli in early spring, also known as Italian broccoli, has loose, leafy stems with no central head. The other type produces a large, dense central flowering head—what you find in grocery stores when you buy a whole broccoli. The head form of broccoli, calabrese, is harvested in summer. If you time planting correctly, you may have a continual harvest throughout spring and fall.

081
PLANT, GROW & HARVEST

SITE Broccoli and cauliflower are cool-season crops that require full sun and rich, well-drained soil.

BEDMATES Broccoli and cauliflower have an upright growth, so they can be planted in rows nearby without shading each other.

CARE Keep well watered. Hand-weed around seedlings. Thin seedlings to 14 to 18 inches (36–46 cm) apart.

HOW TO START Grow broccoli and cauliflower from seeds or seedlings. Start seeds indoors to get a jump on spring planting.

HARVEST Sever broccoli heads with a sharp knife when they're tight and firm, before any buds open into yellow flowers. The tiny yellow flowers that bloom from the florets indicate that broccoli is past its peak, although it is still edible. Cut broccoli stems at an angle to decrease stem rotting; continue to harvest the small side shoots. Once you harvest the head of cauliflower, pull the plant.

PESTS AND DISEASES Broccoli and cauliflower share some of the same pests. Tiny aphids can build colonies on the undersides of the leaves—use insecticidal soap to treat. Cabbage worms or cabbage loopers are the most common pests, attacking leaves and heads. These smooth green caterpillars can destroy an entire harvest if not controlled.

082 TAKE THESE TIPS TO THE GARDEN

PLANT Start seeds indoors ¼ to ½ inch (6–12 mm) deep in very early spring, then transplant into the garden. Or plant nursery-purchased seedlings; position a bit deeper than the containers they are grown in.

TIE Leaves should be tied around cauliflower to keep curd white (A).

HARVEST Cut broccoli and cauliflower at an angle with a sharp knife (B). For cauliflower that needs garden blanching, cover the developing head when it is 2 inches (5 cm) in diameter. Harvest 10 days later when it reaches 6 to 8 inches (15–20 cm) in diameter. For broccoli, harvest while florets are tight and green.

083
KNOW YOUR CAULIFLOWER VARIETIES

'GRAFFITI HYBRID' This variety features bright purple heads that hold color well even when cooked, especially with a little vinegar added to cooking water to make it acidic. They are ready in 85 days.

'SNOW CROWN HYBRID' A standard white variety that's early maturing, widely adapted, and easy to grow in just 55 days.

'VERONICA HYBRID' This romanesco-type produces unique spiky lime green heads in 85 days. They have a mild, nutty flavor.

084
KNOW YOUR BROCCOLI VARIETIES

'ARCADIA' A good disease-resistant variety for areas with foggy or wet conditions. Its tightly packed main head sheds water well and helps prevent rot. 69 days.

'DE CICCO' An Italian heirloom variety that bears a small main head and produces a steady supply of side shoots all season long. 70 days.

'GREEN GOLIATH' This variety produces an 8-inch-diameter (20-cm-diameter) head. 55 days.

'PACKMAN' A head forms in just 52 days and can withstand heat better than most of the broccoli varieties. It adapts well to warm-summer regions.

'SMALL MIRACLE' This variety grows 1 foot (30 cm) tall, a good choice for containers or small-space vegetable gardens. 55 days.

Broccoli, a member of the Brassica family, is a cruciferous vegetable. Its name is derived from the Italian word broccolo, meaning the flowering top of a cabbage.

085
EAT YOUR BROCCOLI IN A PRETTY PASTA

This pappardelle primavera ("spring" in Italian) combines a bushel-basket of seasonal vegetables—including tender broccoli florets—with ribbons of pasta and crunchy toasted hazelnuts.

PREP: 20 minutes   COOK: 20 minutes   MAKES: 4 servings

1	8.8-ounce (250-g) package dried pappardelle pasta
1	cup (125 g) sliced leeks
2	cups (350 g) broccoli florets
1	cup (122 g) bias-sliced carrots (2 medium)
2	cups (190 g) sugar snap pea pods, trimmed
1	cup (187 g) halved grape tomatoes
4	tablespoons butter
2	cloves garlic, minced
½	cup (125 mL) dry white wine
1	to 2 teaspoons snipped fresh thyme
¼	cup (29 g) coarsely chopped toasted hazelnuts
¼	teaspoon salt
⅛	teaspoon black pepper
¼	cup (20 g) shaved Parmesan cheese

STEP 1 In a large pot cook pasta according to package directions; drain. Return pasta to pot. Cover.

STEP 2 Place a steamer basket in a large saucepan. Add water to just below the bottom of the basket; bring to boiling. Add leeks. Cover and steam 2 minutes. Add broccoli and carrots; cover and steam 3 minutes or until crisp-tender. Add pea pods. Cover and steam 1 minute or until crisp-tender. Add vegetables and tomatoes to pot, then recover.

STEP 3 Meanwhile, for sauce, in a medium saucepan combine butter and garlic. Stir over medium heat until butter is melted. Cook 5 minutes or until butter is lightly browned, stirring occasionally. Stir in wine and thyme; heat through.

STEP 4 Add the sauce and nuts to pasta; toss. Season with salt and pepper. Top with cheese.

EACH SERVING *489 cal, 19 g fat, 34 mg chol, 381 mg sodium, 63 g carb, 7 g fiber, 15 g pro*

086
CURRY FAVOR WITH ROASTED CAULIFLOWER

A squeeze of lime is the finishing touch on this absolutely delicious roasted Indian cauliflower. It's flavored with mustard seeds, sugar, fresh ginger, turmeric, cumin, coriander, and crushed red pepper.

PREP: 15 minutes   **ROAST:** 30 minutes at 425°F (220°C)   **MAKES:** 8 servings

2	tablespoons peanut oil
2	teaspoons yellow or black mustard seeds
2	teaspoons sugar
2	teaspoons grated fresh ginger
1½	teaspoons ground turmeric
1½	teaspoons ground cumin
1	teaspoon ground coriander
½	teaspoon salt
¼	teaspoon crushed red pepper
1	medium head cauliflower, cored and cut into florets
2	small bunches baby carrots with tops, tops trimmed
2	tablespoons chopped fresh cilantro
1	lime, cut into 8 wedges

STEP 1 Preheat oven to 425°F (220°C). Line a 15×10×1-inch (38×25×2.5-cm) baking pan with foil; set aside. In a large bowl stir together the first nine ingredients (through red pepper).

STEP 2 Add cauliflower and carrots to bowl; toss to coat. Transfer to prepared baking pan. Roast 30 minutes or until tender and vegetables begin to brown on edges, stirring twice.

STEP 3 Transfer to a serving dish. Sprinkle with cilantro. Serve with lime wedges.

EACH SERVING *71 cal, 4 g fat, 0 mg chol, 188 mg sodium, 8 g carb, 2 g fiber, 2 g pro*

SCALLIONS & LEEKS

The scallion goes by many names: spring onion, salad onion, and green onion. An edible member of the *Allium* genus—whose tangy relatives include tender chives, bulbous storage onions, and mild-mannered leeks—this slender onion has a small white bulb with hollow green foliage. Eat both parts of this plant raw or cooked.

The mildness of scallions (*Allium fistulosum*) allows them to be served raw. A versatile spring and fall crop, green onions take 60 days to grow from seeds. Harvest them once they grow about 1 foot (30 cm) tall or leave in the ground to grow bigger and pick over several weeks.

The leek (*Allium porrum*) looks like an overgrown scallion. The bulb is bigger but not as large as a storage onion. The taste of leeks is sweeter than onions. Plant them in the spring and they will be ready to harvest in late summer or early fall.

Because leeks can tolerate frost, leave them in the ground and use them as you want instead of bringing them indoors for storage. Leeks can be baked, grilled, and used in soups and sauces. They add rich yet subtle flavor to creamy sauces, soups, and stews. They're a must for any food enthusiast's garden—just be sure to wash leeks thoroughly before cooking because the folded leaves capture soil.

087
PLANT, GROW & HARVEST

SITE Plant in a sunny spot in well-drained soil that's rich in organic matter. If you have clay soil, plant bulbs in a raised bed amended with humus.

BEDMATES Plant scallions and leeks with carrots, beets, kohlrabi, strawberries, Brassicas (such as broccoli, cauliflower, and kale), dill, lettuce, and tomatoes.

CARE Keep the soil around scallions and onions consistently moist but not waterlogged. Take care when weeding around young plants. Hand-weeding is best because scallions and leeks have shallow root systems; cultivating tools may harm bulbs. Sidedress by applying fertilizer between the rows of the growing crop.

HOW TO START Direct-seed leeks in the garden a month before the last frost date or start them indoors and transplant outside at the time of the average last frost. Mound soil around stems to exclude light and produce long white shanks.

HARVEST To harvest leeks and green onions, grasp the plant at the top of the bulb and twist the stalks back and forth to loosen them. Then just pop them out of the ground. Cut off the short roots. This frost-hardy plant can be harvested long after many other garden vegetables.

PESTS AND DISEASES Generally scallions and leeks are fairly pest- and disease-free.

088 TAKE THESE TIPS TO THE GARDEN

HAND-PULL Because scallions and leeks have shallow roots, it is best to pull weeds by hand to protect their shallow-rooted bulbs (A).

PLANT Leeks should be planted in early spring (B).

HARVEST Leeks are ready to harvest when they are 1 to 2 inches (3–5 cm) in diameter at the base (C).

090
KNOW YOUR SCALLION VARIETIES

'EVERGREEN HARDY WHITE' Plant this perennial in spring or fall. It's ready to harvest 65 days after a spring planting.

'PARADE' This variety produces 12- to 16-inch (30–41 cm) green onions, ready to harvest in 60 days.

091
KNOW YOUR LEEK VARIETIES

'GIANT MUSSELBURGH' This Scottish heirloom variety produces 2- to 3-inch-thick (5–8 cm) stems. It is exceptionally cold-tolerant. 100 days.

'KING RICHARD' Tall and thin, this variety matures just 75 days after transplanting.

089
MAXIMIZE YOUR YIELD

Because they're harvested while still young, green onions can be planted fairly close together, about 1 to 2 inches (3–5 cm). If you grow onions longer to form bulbs, space them 2 to 3 inches (5–8 cm) apart. You might want to harvest every other green onion and leave the rest to grow and mature.

If you only want to use the green tops of scallions, try regrowing the greens with this trick (foliage can be easily regrown from the white bulb): Place the white bulb, roots down, in a glass or jar with just enough water to cover the roots. Place in a sunny location. Change the water every couple of days. You can reuse the green leafy parts for a couple of weeks until they lose flavor.

092
TRY A LEEK TART

The layers of leeks can hold a lot of dirt. To clean before cooking, trim and discard the root end and dark green leaves, then cut the white and light green part in half lengthwise. Fanning the layers, rinse under cool running water.

PREP: 30 minutes   **BAKE:** 20 minutes at 375°F (190°C)   **COOL:** 10 minutes   **MAKES:** 12 servings

2	tablespoons olive oil
3	cups (375 g) thinly sliced leeks (4 to 6 medium leeks)
4	cloves garlic, minced
½	cup (175 g) chopped red sweet pepper
2	tablespoons Dijon-style mustard
1	teaspoon dried herbes de Provence or dried basil, crushed
6	ounces (170 g) Gruyère cheese or Swiss cheese, shredded
1	15-ounce (425-g) package rolled refrigerated unbaked piecrust (2 crusts)
2	tablespoons milk
2	tablespoons chopped almonds or walnuts

STEP 1 Preheat oven to 375°F (190°C). In a large skillet heat oil over medium heat. Add leeks and garlic to hot oil; cook 5 minutes or until tender. Remove from heat; stir in sweet pepper, mustard, and herbes de Provence. Cool slightly; stir in cheese.

STEP 2 On a baking sheet unroll one piecrust according to package directions. Roll into a 12-inch (30-cm) circle. Spoon half the leek mixture into the center of piecrust, leaving a 2-inch (5-cm) border. Fold the border up over leek mixture. Brush milk onto top and sides of crust. Sprinkle with 1 tablespoon of the nuts. Repeat with remaining piecrust, filling, milk, and nuts.

STEP 3 Bake 20 to 25 minutes or until crusts are golden. Cool 10 minutes on baking sheets. Cut each tart into 12 wedges. Serve warm or at room temperature.

EACH SERVING *132 cal, 9 g fat, 11 mg chol, 99 mg sodium, 11 g carb, 0 g fiber, 3 g pro*

093
FLAVOR COUSCOUS WITH GREEN ONIONS

Whether you call them green onions or scallions, these delicate onions give color and flavor to this veggie-packed warm couscous dressed in a lime vinaigrette.

PREP: 15 minutes   COOK: 8 minutes   MAKES: 4 servings

1	10-ounce (283-g) package couscous
2	cups (256 g) coarsely chopped carrots
1	tablespoon olive oil
2	medium zucchini and/or yellow summer squash, quartered lengthwise and cut into ½-inch (12-mm) pieces
6	green onions, cut into 1-inch (3-cm) pieces
½	cup (125 mL) lime or lemon juice
¼	cup (50 mL) olive oil
1	tablespoon honey
1	teaspoon salt
½	teaspoon black pepper
½	cup (58 g) chopped walnuts, toasted*
2	ounces (57 g) Parmigiano-Reggiano cheese, shaved

STEP 1 Prepare couscous according to package directions.

STEP 2 Meanwhile, in a large skillet cook and stir carrots in hot oil 2 minutes. Add zucchini and green onions; cook and stir about 6 minutes or just until vegetables are tender. Transfer couscous to a bowl and fluff with a fork. Add carrot mixture.

STEP 3 In a screw-top jar combine lime juice, oil, honey, salt, and pepper. Cover and shake well. Pour over couscous mixture; toss. Top with walnuts and cheese.

*TIP To toast walnuts, preheat oven to 350°F (175°C). Spread walnuts in a shallow baking pan. Bake 5 to 10 minutes or until nuts are lightly browned, shaking pan once or twice.

EACH SERVING *643 cal, 31 g fat, 10 mg chol, 884 mg sodium, 75 g carb, 8 g fiber, 19 g pro*

CHAPTER 3

Summer

TOMATOES

There are two types of tomatoes: determinate and indeterminate. Determinate tomatoes are compact and produce clusters of flowers at the growing tip. The plants set fruit along the stem within 2 to 3 weeks, and the fruits ripen almost simultaneously, producing a heavy crop all at once. Many paste and early-season tomatoes are determinate; most paste tomatoes are used for cooking because of low moisture content. Indeterminate tomatoes continue to grow throughout the season because the terminal end of the stem produces leaves instead of flowers. New flowers appear continuously along the side shoots and bloom as long as growing conditions are favorable, producing a steady supply of tomatoes all season.

Heirloom tomatoes are nearly as easy to grow as conventional tomatoes. Thanks to preservation efforts of generations of tomato lovers, seeds and transplants are easy to find online and through mail-order sources. While the origins of many varieties are no longer known, heritage is safely preserved in the taste, color, shape, and texture of the fruit. Heirloom tomatoes, like other fruits, vegetables, and flowers tagged with the "heirloom" label, are open-pollinated, meaning wind, insects, or the plants themselves take care of producing the next genetic mutation. The result is offspring that look and, in the case of tomatoes, taste just like their parents.

094
PLANT, GROW & HARVEST

SITE Tomatoes grow best in highly fertile, well-drained, slightly acid soil. Add amendments to improve the planting site. Tomato seeds can be sown directly in the soil, but most home gardeners purchase seedlings to plant in a sunny location after the last frost date. Plant small bush tomatoes 1½ to 2 feet (46–61 cm) apart, and larger types 3 to 4 feet (0.91–1.2 m) apart if not staked.

BEDMATES Grow indeterminate and determinate tomatoes together.

CARE In hot climates new transplants may need to be shaded until they are established. Place stakes or cages at planting time to avoid injuring roots later. Train indeterminate plants up stakes or grow them inside wire cages for air circulation and to keep fruit off the ground. Remove suckers just beyond the first two leaves that develop.

HOW TO START Grow from seeds or plant seedlings.

HARVEST Pick tomatoes when they have reached full variety size and color. Tomatoes continue ripening off the plant.

PESTS AND DISEASES Tomatoes are susceptible to a wide variety of diseases caused by environmental stress. Grow healthy plants by choosing varieties bred for resistance to disease and tolerance of problems common to your area.

095 TAKE THESE TIPS TO THE GARDEN

PLANT Transplants should be planted into the garden 2 weeks after the average last-frost date in your area. Promote strong plants and an ample root system by planting deeply. Set plants into the ground up to their first set of leaves (A).

STAKE Cage or stake plants soon after planting to give them support and keep fruit off the ground (B).

WATER Plants should be watered deeply during extended dry periods. Tomato plants are resourceful and mine for water. Supplemental watering during drought periods helps plants fend off pests and form fruit (C).

GROW If you don't have room for a full-size garden, grow tomatoes in containers (D).

> *With hundreds of excellent heirloom tomatoes to choose from, you can spend summer after summer trying them all. Heirlooms are some of the most flavorful, problem-free, and productive varieties.*

096
KNOW YOUR VARIETIES

'BOX CAR WILLIE' A prolific producer covered with clusters of round, red fruits. It has robust tomato flavor and ripens in midseason.

'SOLDACKI' Fruits are meaty and ripen to deep pink or red with sweet flavor. A high-yielding plant, it ripens in midseason.

'ROSE' (RUSSIAN ROSE) A meaty, dusty rose heirloom with sweet tomato flavor.

'BEAM'S YELLOW PEAR' These sweet yellow pear-shape tomatoes make the perfect snack.

'CHEROKEE PURPLE' This variety has a rich, smoky-sweet taste, making it one of the best purple-skin tomatoes.

'AUNT RUBY'S GERMAN GREEN' A green beefsteak tomato with spicy-sweet flavor.

'ITALIAN HEIRLOOM' Big red fruits, rich tomato flavor, and large fruit in an all-purpose variety.

'NYAGOUS' The baseball-size fruits yield silky purple-black skin that encloses flavorful purple flesh.

'BRANDYWINE' One of the most popular and readily available heirloom tomatoes.

'GREEN ZEBRA' Round and olive yellow tomatoes with deep green stripes and tangy-sweet flavor.

'MEXICO MIDGET' Hundreds of cherry-size tomatoes are produced from mid-summer until frost.

097
TOSS A TINY TOMATO SALAD

These small-scale fruits are tossed with fennel, arugula, and a tasty champagne vinaigrette. For the prettiest salad, use a variety of colors and shapes—pear, cherry, and grape tomatoes in shades of red, yellow, and orange.

START TO FINISH: 20 minutes   MAKES: 12 servings

4	cups (552 g) assorted tiny tomatoes
2	cups (20 g) arugula or watercress
1	small fennel bulb, quartered, cored, and very thinly sliced
⅓	cup (10 g) chopped fresh Italian parsley
¼	cup (25 g) finely chopped shallots
¼	cup (50 mL) olive oil
3	tablespoons champagne vinegar
1	teaspoon lemon zest
¼	teaspoon salt
⅛	teaspoon black pepper

STEP 1 In a salad bowl toss together tomatoes, arugula, fennel, and parsley.

STEP 2 For dressing, in a screw-top jar combine shallots, oil, vinegar, lemon zest, salt, and pepper. Cover and shake well. Pour dressing over tomato salad.

EACH SERVING *58 cal, 5 g fat, 0 mg chol, 58 mg sodium, 4 g carb, 1 g fiber, 1 g pro*

098
TRY A TOMATO TART

A galette is a rustic French-style tart that can be sweet or savory. Here, slices of juicy heirloom tomatoes are arranged in a Parmesan-black pepper crust, topped with goat cheese, and baked until bubbly.

PREP: 35 minutes   CHILL: 30 minutes   STAND: 30 minutes   BAKE: 30 minutes at 375°F (190°C)   COOL: 10 minutes   MAKES: 8 servings

½   cup (115 g) cold unsalted butter, cubed

1½   cups (213 g) all-purpose flour

⅓   cup (33 g) shredded Parmesan cheese

1   teaspoon cracked black pepper

4   to 6 tablespoons cold water

4   large heirloom tomatoes, cored, approximately 2 pounds (1 kg)

1   teaspoon kosher salt

3   tablespoons fine dry bread crumbs

½   cup (50 g) thinly sliced shallots

2   teaspoons fresh thyme leaves

4   to 6 ounces (115–170 g) semisoft goat cheese (chèvre)

1   egg, lightly beaten

Fresh basil leaves

STEP 1 In a large bowl cut butter into flour with a pastry blender until pieces are pea-size. Stir in Parmesan and cracked pepper.

STEP 2 Sprinkle 1 tablespoon cold water over part of the flour; toss with a fork. Push moistened dough to the side. Repeat until all dough is moistened. Form dough into a disk, wrap with plastic wrap, and chill 30 minutes.

STEP 3 Meanwhile, slice the tomatoes ¼ inch (6 mm) thick and arrange on a wire rack over a baking pan. Sprinkle with salt; let stand 30 minutes.

STEP 4 Preheat oven to 375°F (190°C). Line a large baking sheet with parchment paper. On a lightly floured surface, roll dough to a 13-inch (33-cm) circle. Transfer to the baking sheet.

STEP 5 Spread bread crumbs on pastry, leaving a 2-inch (5-cm) border. Layer tomatoes, shallots, thyme, and goat cheese on crumbs. Fold border over filling. Combine egg and 1 tablespoon water; brush over edges of pastry.

STEP 6 Bake 30 to 40 minutes or until crust is browned. Cool 10 minutes. Serve with basil.

EACH SERVING *300 cal, 18 g fat, 67 mg chol, 414 mg sodium, 26 g carb, 3 g fiber, 9 g pro*

HERBS

Culinary herbs reflect food cultures. Cooks use what grows well and is plentiful in the regions where they live. For example, the unique flavor of Mediterranean food relies on herbs that grow well during the long, sunny days and dry climates of Italy, southern France, and Greece. In addition to creating authentic dishes with fresh herbs, people enjoy myriad shades of green, a range of textures, and delightful fragrances of well-established and easy-to-care-for herb gardens. There are many classic herb garden designs—of all sizes. Little space is needed to grow herbs; they grow as well in containers as in the ground. Many gardeners who have space to plant a formal herb garden also keep herbs in containers close to the kitchen door to use in cooking, as garnishes, or for crafts.

If you have space for a full kitchen garden, plant herbs that you and your family love: basil for pesto, rosemary for pizzas, cilantro for salsa. Once you get used to picking fresh herbs to use in the kitchen, you'll be hooked.

Growing herbs from seeds or cuttings is very economical. Herb plants are sold in nearly every garden center too. Generally herbs enjoy fertile soil and (for most herbs) a sunny site. Frequent harvesting keeps plants lush and productive throughout the growing season. There are annual and perennial herbs, and some herbs can be grown indoors during late fall and winter.

099
PLANT, GROW & HARVEST

SITE Most herbs grow best in a sunny spot in well-drained soil.

BEDMATES Herbs grow well with other herbs. Low-growing herbs, such as parsley and thyme, are excellent flowerbed edging plants.

CARE Go light on fertilizer, using organic sources that supply nutrients slowly. Feeding herbs a steady diet of nutrients robs them of their essential oils—the essence that makes them so valuable in the kitchen. Herbs develop the most intense flavor when kept on the dry side.

HOW TO START Start from seeds or cuttings or transplant small herb plants directly into the ground or a container. The best time to plant an herb depends on its cold tolerance and the average last frost date in your area. Sow hardy perennial herb seeds outdoors several weeks before the average last frost date. Most tender annual herbs germinate better in warm soil—so wait until after the average last frost date to plant them.

HARVEST Throughout summer, snip plants regularly to encourage branching and new growth. Harvest successive cuttings whenever you need fresh herbs. Generally cut no more than one-third of the stem length. Exceptions include chives and lavender: When they bloom, harvest the flowering stems at ground level.

100 TAKE THESE TIPS TO THE GARDEN

TRANSPLANT Herbs can be planted into individual 6-inch (15-cm) pots or large decorative containers that can hold several plants. Create a mini herb garden in a container that is at least 12 inches (30 cm) in diameter. Herbs with Mediterranean origins, such as oregano, thyme, and rosemary, prefer soil on the dry side (A).

THE POT Fill the pot with potting soil. Press the potted herb into the soil to make a planting hole just the right size

and depth. Gently slip the young plant out of its nursery pot. Squeeze the root ball to loosen it (B).

THE ROOT BALL Set the root ball in the planting hole, with the plant at the same level or slightly deeper than it was in its nursery pot. Lightly press soil around the plant. Fill a larger pot with several plants, repeating the process for each. Water the soil thoroughly. If needed, top off with more soil, leaving 1 inch (2.5 cm) between the top of the soil and top of the pot to allow for watering (C).

101
KNOW YOUR VARIETIES

BASIL Common sweet basil has flat green leaves and a minty flavor; other varieties have purplish, reddish, or ruffled leaves.

CHIVES The slender, hollow leaves have a delicate onion flavor.

CILANTRO/CORIANDER A two-in-one herb: The leaves are cilantro and the seeds are coriander.

DILL Easily grows from seed in full sun or light shade. Harvest leaves just before flowers open.

LAVENDER A pretty herb with an intense floral fragrance when its grayish foliage is pinched.

OREGANO In full sun and sandy, well-drained soil, this perennial grows to 2 feet (61 cm) tall.

TARRAGON The leaves have sweet, aniselike flavor.

MINT Grow mint from cuttings or allow shoots to root in water or damp soil. Seed-grown mints lack leaf flavor.

PARSLEY Available in two varieties, curly-leaf (used mainly as a garnish) and flat-leaf or Italian.

ROSEMARY This beautiful perennial grows as a medium-size shrub in warm climates.

SAGE A slight lemony flavor when fresh, sage has a stronger, mustier flavor when dried.

THYME With dozens of flavors and colors, this plant will attract bees to your garden.

102
GO GOURMET WITH HERB BUTTER

Crunchy radish slices with salt on buttered baguette is a classic French appetizer. This recipe ups the ante with fresh herbs in the butter and smoked salt for sprinkling.

START TO FINISH: 30 minutes MAKES: 8 servings

- ½ cup (115 g) unsalted butter, softened
- 2 tablespoons finely chopped green onion
- 1 tablespoon snipped fresh basil
- 2 teaspoons snipped fresh Italian parsley
- 1 teaspoon snipped fresh thyme
- 1 teaspoon lemon zest
- ⅛ teaspoon freshly ground black pepper
- 8 ounces (225 g) baguette-style French bread, diagonally sliced ¼ inch (6 mm) thick
- 2 bunches assorted radishes with stems
- 2 teaspoons smoked sea salt or coarse sea salt

STEP 1 Preheat oven to 425°F (220°C). In a medium bowl stir together butter, green onion, basil, parsley, thyme, lemon zest, and pepper. Set aside.

STEP 2 Arrange bread slices on a baking sheet. Bake 4 to 5 minutes or until lightly toasted, turning once. Allow bread to cool. Spread cooled toasts with herbed butter. Arrange bread slices on a platter. Set aside.

STEP 3 Stem and thinly slice about 5 radishes. Just before serving, top bread slices with sliced radishes. Add remaining radishes to the platter. Sprinkle toasts with

salt. If desired, serve with a small bowl of sea salt for dipping whole radishes.

EACH SERVING *180 cal, 12 g fat, 31 mg chol, 591 mg sodium, 16 g carb, 1 g fiber, 3 g pro*

103
PREPARE A TASTY TOMATO-HERB PASTA

In the peak of summer, when your herb garden is going strong, make this savory pasta that features five herbs and ricotta salata—a nicely tart, slightly crumbly aged version of fresh ricotta.

PREP: 20 minutes   COOK: 13 minutes   MAKES: 6 servings

8   ounces (225 g) dried penne pasta
2   tablespoons extra-virgin olive oil
⅓   cup (5 g) snipped fresh basil
1   teaspoon snipped fresh oregano
1   teaspoon fresh thyme leaves
½   teaspoon cracked black pepper
4   cups (550 g) grape tomatoes
2   cloves garlic, minced
½   cup (125 mL) vegetable broth
¼   cup (6 g) snipped fresh Italian parsley
2   tablespoons snipped fresh chives
1½   cups (336 g) crumbled ricotta salata or feta cheese

STEP 1 Cook pasta according to package directions; drain well. Transfer drained pasta to a large bowl. Add 1 tablespoon of the oil and the next 4 ingredients (through pepper). Toss to combine; cover to keep warm.

STEP 2 In an extra-large skillet heat the remaining 1 tablespoon oil. Add tomatoes and garlic; cook and stir over medium-high heat 5 to 6 minutes or until tomatoes caramelize, skins burst, and tomatoes begin to break down. Stir in broth; bring to boiling.

STEP 3 Add tomato mixture, parsley, and chives to pasta mixture; toss gently to combine. Top servings

with ricotta salata.

EACH SERVING *287 cal, 11 g fat, 25 mg chol, 569 mg sodium, 34 g carb, 3 g fiber, 11 g pro*

SWEET CORN

Sweet corn (*Zea mays saccharata*) is treasured for its taste. The sweet factor is the primary reason to grow ears in your backyard because freshly picked sweet corn tastes so much better than that from a stand or market. Sweet corn converts sugar to starch the very second it's picked; heirloom varieties are especially quick to lose sweetness, so pick and prepare them immediately.

Corn is the tallest vegetable in the garden with stalks growing more than 6 feet (1.8 m). This fast-growing plant (actually a grass) usually produces one ear per stalk; but in the best conditions, it produces a second ear. Sweet corn varieties have white, yellow, or bicolor kernels.

Sweet corn, although easy to grow, does take space. Plant a 10×10-foot (3×3-m) plot to ensure proper pollination. With corn, planting more is better because you'll get bigger harvests as well as higher-quality ears. Sweet corn is wind pollinated and needs multiple plants for optimal production. An efficient way to plant corn is in blocks of short rows rather than long rows. Even in small areas, you can grow sweet corn successfully. Small corn varieties grow well in compact gardens—you can even grow sweet corn in containers. Plan for a continuous supply by stagger-planting a mix of early-, mid-, and late-season varieties for the longest harvest season.

104
PLANT, GROW & HARVEST

SITE Corn needs a planting location that receives full sun. Soil should have good drainage.

BEDMATES Don't plant different varieties of corn next to each other; they will pollinate each other. Rotate corn crops every year.

CARE Corn loves good soil. Add nutrients by using compost or manure. To fertilize plants, use high-nitrogen fertilizer mixes. Sidedress with 33-0-0 plant food.

HOW TO START Start seeds 6 to 8 weeks before your average last frost date. Use fresh seed every year. Yellow and white corn varieties can cross-pollinate, which may turn white corn to yellow.

HARVEST With a sharp downward twist, break the shank or stem below the ear without breaking the parent stalk. Cook and eat the ears immediately or prepare them for freezing or canning as soon as possible. To preserve sweetness, refrigerate ears after picking.

PESTS AND DISEASES Sweet corn can be affected by leaf blight, corn smut, and bacterial wilt; choose varieties that are resistant to diseases that occur in your garden. Flea beetles can cause bacterial wilt; protect young plants using floating row covers. Control earworm on early and midseason varieties with insecticide spray. Mature ears may be attractive to raccoons or deer. A fence around your plot will deter these thieves.

105 TAKE THESE TIPS TO THE GARDEN

SOW Once the soil has warmed, sow seeds in the ground. Space seeds 8 to 12 inches (20–30 cm) apart.

PLANT Corn should be planted in blocks of three or more plants instead of in rows to provide support for stalks and help encourage pollination.

WEEDS Remove weeds by hand or hoe shallowly to avoid damaging close-to-the-surface roots (A).

WATER During drought times, water to help ear development (B).

HARVEST When the silks of the ear begin to turn brown at the tips, peel back some of the husk to check for maturity (C). Perfect sweet corn kernels should be milky. Immature kernels are watery. When sweet corn is past maturity, kernels are tough and doughy.

106
EAT SWEET

Supersweet sweet corn varieties are slower to convert to starch than regular sweet corn; that's why they're sweet. These cultivars take time to germinate and have reduced seedling vigor, so it's best to wait to plant until soil has warmed to at least 60°F (16°C). Supersweet sweet corn varieties should be isolated from other types of corn as cross pollination with regular corn results in starchy kernels. Plant at least 250 feet (76 m) away from other types of corn. Another option is to stagger planting dates or select cultivars that mature at different times so tasseling periods don't overlap. Plant at least two weeks apart, or use varieties with at least 14 days' difference in maturity.

107
KNOW YOUR VARIETIES

Choose from standard sugary (SU), sugar-enhanced (SE), and supersweet (Sh2) varieties with yellow, white, or bicolor kernels. SU is the least sweet but full of rich flavor and offers high yields. SE offers the highest sugar content and best tenderness but is not as stress-tolerant as SU varieties. Sh2 features two to three times the sugar, but plants are less vigorous than other hybrids.

'SILVER QUEEN' A white standard sugary variety that's a longtime favorite. It matures in 92 days.

'ILLINI XTRA SWEET' A yellow supersweet variety that matures in 85 days. It freezes well.

'PEACHES 'N CREAM' Hybrid is a bicolor, sugar-enhanced variety that produces small creamy, tender kernels. Matures in just 70 days.

'BONUS' This hybrid is a baby-type corn that produces three to six small ears on each stalk just 35 days after planting. Use this baby corn in Asian dishes.

'GOLDEN MIDGET' This variety is ideal for small gardens. Stalks are 3 feet (91 cm) tall. Its 4-inch (10-cm) ears are ready to eat in 60 days.

'GOLD BANTAM' A yellow heirloom variety known for sweetness. Cook within several hours of harvest for the best flavor.

'MANDAN RED FLOUR' This variety has 6-inch (15-cm) ears with pale yellow kernels that mature to deep red when dry.

108
GO NATIVE WITH SUCCOTASH SALAD

This fresh and crunchy adaptation of a traditional Native American dish of corn and beans is dressed in a creamy buttermilk avocado dressing and topped with crumbled bacon.

PREP: 25 minutes   COOK: 20 minutes   MAKES: 4 servings

2	ears fresh sweet corn
1	cup (75 g) fresh lima beans
¾	cup (175 mL) buttermilk
½	avocado, seeded, and peeled
1	tablespoon snipped fresh Italian parsley
¼	teaspoon salt
¼	teaspoon onion powder
¼	teaspoon dry mustard
¼	teaspoon black pepper
1	clove garlic, minced
1	large head butterhead (Boston or Bibb) lettuce, torn
2	cups (250 g) sliced grilled chicken breast*
6	slices bacon, crisp-cooked and crumbled
½	cup (80 g) finely chopped red onion
½	cup (60 g) crumbled blue or feta cheese

STEP 1 Cut corn kernels from cobs; set kernels aside. In a small saucepan bring 1 cup (250 mL) of lightly salted water to boiling. Add lima beans and simmer 15 minutes or until tender. Remove with a slotted spoon; set aside. Add corn to saucepan. Simmer 3 minutes or until tender; drain.

STEP 2 For dressing, in a blender combine buttermilk, avocado, parsley, salt, onion powder, dry mustard, pepper, and garlic. Cover and blend until smooth. Pour into a small pitcher.

STEP 3 Line a large platter with lettuce. Arrange chicken, crumbled bacon, corn, lima beans, onion, and cheese in rows on lettuce. Serve with dressing.

*TIP To grill chicken, lightly season 12 ounces (340 g) of skinless, boneless chicken breast halves with salt and pepper. Grill over medium heat 12 to 15 minutes or until chicken is no longer pink (170°F/77°C), turning once.

EACH SERVING *375 cal, 15 g fat, 87 mg chol, 692 mg sodium, 24 g carb, 5 g fiber, 36 g pro*

109
WHIP UP A WILD RICE & ROASTED CORN PILAF

Wild rice is actually not rice at all but rather the seed of an aquatic grass. Its nutty flavor goes perfectly with the toasty-sweet taste of roasted corn in this hearty pilaf.

PREP: 20 minutes   COOK: 40 minutes   GRILL: 7 minutes   MAKES: 4 servings

½   cup (178 g) wild rice, rinsed and drained

4   ears fresh sweet corn, husks and silks removed

    Nonstick cooking spray

1   15-ounce (425-g) can garbanzo beans (chickpeas), rinsed and drained

½   cup (63 g) chopped toasted* walnuts

⅓   cup (5 g) chopped fresh basil

3   tablespoons olive oil

3   tablespoons lime juice

½   teaspoon salt

¼   teaspoon black pepper

1   avocado, halved, seeded, peeled, and sliced or chopped

    Mixed greens

    Lime wedges (optional)

STEP 1 In a large saucepan bring 1½ cups (375 mL) water to boiling; stir in rice. Reduce heat; simmer, covered, about 40 minutes or until kernels open. Meanwhile, coat corn with cooking spray. Grill, uncovered, over medium-high heat 7 to 8 minutes or until charred, turning frequently. Remove from grill; cut slabs of kernels from corn cobs.

STEP 2 Drain rice, if necessary. Carefully stir in corn, garbanzo beans, walnuts, basil, oil, lime juice, salt, and pepper. Return to low heat; heat through.

STEP 3 Serve the mixed greens alongside the pilaf and avocado. Serve with lime wedges if desired.

*TIP To toast walnuts, preheat oven to 350°F (175°C). Spread walnuts in a shallow baking pan. Bake 5 to 10 minutes or until nuts are lightly browned, shaking pan once or twice.

EACH SERVING *474 cal, 28 g fat, 0 mg chol, 430 mg sodium, 51 g carb, 10 g fiber, 13 g pro*

PEPPERS

Botanically classified as fruits, peppers are primarily served as vegetables and seasoning. Chile (or hot) peppers are fruits of the genus *Capsicum*. Usually grown as annuals, peppers are perennials that originated in the Amazon basin and one of the most versatile vegetables in the garden. They are available in a range of heat and flavor levels—from mild sweet peppers to fiery habaneros. Peppers grow in many shapes, including round, oblong, and nearly square. And colors! Peppers grow in a rainbow of hues—green, red, yellow, and purple.

Growing peppers is easy. Plant them in the ground or grow them in containers. As tropical hot-weather plants, they thrive in heat. Always position them in a sunny spot. In addition to culinary peppers, many bright-color ornamental peppers make beautiful container plants.

If you're into peppers for heat, plant the hottest varieties: Ancho or poblano peppers are mildly hot; jalapeños are several times hotter. Tabasco peppers are up to 50 times hotter and habaneros are 100 times hotter. Pepper heat varies within the same variety—and even the same pod. The heat-producing substance, capsaicin, increases when plants lack water, when pods mature, and when peppers ripen in high temperatures. Capsaicin is concentrated most in pepper ribs, crosswalls, and stems.

110
PLANT, GROW & HARVEST

SITE Peppers need a sunny location—at least 6 hours of sun a day. Because peppers are hot-weather vegetables, choose a location where temperature is 70 to 75°F (21–24°C) in the daytime and no lower than 60°F (16°C) at night.

BEDMATES Many plants are good companions for peppers, including herbs, radishes, lettuces, greens, carrots, cucumbers, and onions.

CARE Keep soil well-drained, but maintain adequate moisture. Water 1 to 2 inches (2.5–5 cm) per week. If the climate is very warm or dry, watering peppers every day may be necessary.

HOW TO START Start peppers from seeds indoors in late winter then transplant into the garden after the soil and air have warmed. Start indoors 40 to 60 days before transplanting time. Or purchase pepper seedlings.

HARVEST Most sweet peppers mature in 60 to 90 days; hot peppers take longer to mature—up to 150 days.

PESTS AND DISEASES Gardeners who grow or use tobacco are liable to spread tobacco mosaic disease to pepper plants and should wash their hands with soap and water before handling pepper plants. Aphids will also attack peppers. Look for them on the underside of leaves and near new growth. Use insecticidal soap to treat.

111 TAKE THESE TIPS TO THE GARDEN

STAKE Young pepper plants need support to keep them upright and for support once they start producing fruit (A).

DRIP IRRIGATION Install drip irrigation to make watering easy. Drip systems are the most efficient way to water (B).

WEED Carefully hoe (or hand-pull) weeds around pepper plants to keep them from encroaching and robbing soil of nutrients and water.

MULCH To conserve moisture and control weed germination, top soil with mulch.

PLANT To avoid cross-pollination, plant sweet and hot pepper varieties as far apart as possible in the garden.

PEPPERS Pick peppers often to increase yields. Harvest peppers before they mature to keep crops producing fruit. Cut off peppers with scissors or pruning shears to avoid tearing the stems (C).

113
KNOW YOUR SWEET PEPPER VARIETIES

'ACE HYBRID' This red pepper matures early and grows well in cool climates.

'ADMIRAL' This plant bears blocky fruits that turn from green to yellow at maturity. Matures in 80 days from planting.

'CALIFORNIA WONDER' A thick-walled sweet pepper used for stuffing.

'CARMEN' This variety produces a sweet bull-horn-type pepper that turns from green to red when ripe.

'GOLDEN BELL HYBRID' This thick-walled pepper turns from green to deep gold at maturity.

'GYPSY' This early-maturing sweet pepper features elongated fruits that turn pale yellow to orange to red.

'SWEET BANANA' Named for its mild, sweet flesh and elongated yellow immature form. At maturity it turns red.

112
KNOW YOUR HOT PEPPER VARIETIES

Although pepper variety determines heat, weather also plays a role in flavor. Plants that get less water produce fewer but hotter peppers. And cool, cloudy weather makes peppers less hot.

'ANCHO 211' Mildly hot heart-shape fruits, good for stuffing and drying.

'HOLY MOLE' A mildly hot pepper developed especially for mole sauce. Green fruits mature to chocolate brown.

'PRETTY IN PURPLE' This variety offers edible hot attractive purple fruits, stems, and leaves.

'THAI HOT' This variety bears extremely hot pencil-thin fruits.

'CAYENNE' Fruits of this variety are long, slim, and very hot.

'JALAPEÑO' This popular variety produces dark green, medium-hot peppers. Matures to dark red.

'TABASCO' The peppers of this plant are used to make the sauce with the same name.

114
CHOW DOWN ON SWEET PEPPER CHOWDER

Charring sweet peppers for this creamy potato chowder will caramelize the natural sugars, making them even sweeter—and it adds pretty bits of color to the soup.

PREP: 20 minutes   COOK: 32 minutes   MAKES: 4 servings

Nonstick cooking spray

3   cups (525 g) chopped red
     sweet peppers

2   cups (300 g) chopped
     yellow onions

1¾   cups (395 g) chopped peeled
     russet potatoes

½   cup (125 mL) vegetable broth

2   cups (475 mL) milk

⅛   teaspoon cayenne pepper
     (optional)

1   tablespoon butter

¼   cup (6 g) snipped fresh parsley
     Salt and black pepper

½   cup (50 g) shredded white or
     sharp cheddar cheese (optional)

¼   cup (56 g) plain Greek yogurt
     (optional)

     Crumbled crisp-cooked bacon
     (optional)

STEP 1 Coat a Dutch oven with cooking spray; heat over medium-high heat. Add sweet peppers; coat with cooking spray. Cook, uncovered, about 15 minutes or until charred, stirring frequently.

STEP 2 Add onions; cook 5 to 6 minutes or until soft and golden brown, stirring occasionally. Stir in potatoes and broth. Bring to boiling, reduce heat. Simmer, covered, for 12 minutes or until potatoes are very tender. Coarsely mash pepper mixture. Stir in milk and, if using, cayenne pepper. Heat through.

STEP 3 Remove from heat; stir in butter and parsley. Season to taste with salt and black pepper. If desired, top individual servings with cheese, yogurt, bacon, and/or additional parsley.

EACH SERVING *255 cal, 11 g fat, 32 mg chol, 284 mg sodium, 30 g carb, 5 g fiber, 11 g pro*

115
STUFF SOME SWEET PEPPERS

These farro-stuffed peppers take advantage of peak-of-summer sweet corn in the filling. Use vegetable broth instead of chicken broth and they're vegetarian.

PREP: 20 minutes   COOK: 35 minutes   BAKE: 45 minutes at 400°F (200°C)   MAKES: 4 servings

1	14.5-ounce (411-g) can reduced-sodium vegetable chicken broth
1	cup (52 g) farro
1	cup (250 mL) water
2	ears fresh sweet corn
2	tablespoons butter or olive oil
1	teaspoon curry powder
½	cup (45 g) sliced green onions
1	cup (150 g) chopped yellow summer squash and/or zucchini
¼	teaspoon salt
¼	teaspoon black pepper
8	ounces (225 g) fontina cheese, shredded
½	cup (8 g) snipped fresh basil
4	large red sweet peppers

STEP 1 In a medium saucepan combine broth, farro, and water. Bring to boiling. Reduce heat, cover, and simmer 30 minutes or until farro is tender. Drain farro, reserving ½ cup (125 mL) of the cooking liquid.

STEP 2 Preheat oven to 400°F (200°C). Remove husks and silks from corn. Cut corn from cobs, discarding cobs. In a large skillet melt the butter over medium heat. Stir in curry powder. Add reserved corn and green onions. Cook 2 minutes, stirring occasionally. Add squash and cook 2 minutes more. Stir in reserved farro, salt, and black pepper; cool slightly. Stir in half the cheese and half the basil.

STEP 3 Cut sweet peppers in half lengthwise. Remove and discard seeds and membranes. Fill pepper halves with farro mixture. Place stuffed peppers in a 3-quart (3 L) baking dish. Pour the reserved liquid into dish around peppers. Cover dish with foil.

STEP 4 Bake 30 minutes. Remove foil. Sprinkle with remaining cheese. Bake, uncovered, 15 minutes or until peppers are crisp-tender and cheese is melted. Sprinkle with remaining basil.

EACH SERVING *536 cal, 25 g fat, 81 mg chol, 943 mg sodium, 53 g carb, 7 g fiber, 25 g pro*

SUMMER SQUASH

Prolific and delicious, summer squash (*Cucurbita pepo*) varieties produce pound after pound of colorful and sculptural edibles. These beauties can be long, straight, and thin like traditional zucchini or feature a swollen base with a thin, bent top like crookneck. They can be shaped like a baseball, such as round zucchini. And pattypan can resemble a flying saucer. Botanically, squash are a fruit, though we treat them as a vegetable.

The classic long, narrow, green zucchini is probably the most well-known of the summer squashes. Its smooth skin, meaty flesh, and mild taste make it ideal for cooking.

Other summer squashes—crooknecks and pattypan—are multipurpose vegetables: to slice or chop into salads, to add texture and heft to soups (simmer lightly to preserve texture), or to combine with other vegetables.

Summer squash plants are notoriously prolific. Only one or two may supply enough for your needs. Before plants start pumping out the goods, you may harvest blossoms for soups or frying. Edible blossoms star in recipes for fried squash blossoms or squash blossom soup.

Summer squash differs from fall and winter squash. These vegetables are harvested before the rind hardens and the soft rind can be left on to eat.

116
PLANT, GROW & HARVEST

SITE Summer squash require sun with a lot of space.

BEDMATES Plant with beans or corn; don't plant near potatoes.

CARE If you plant seeds, thin emerging seedlings to three plants per hill. Water squash plants regularly.

HOW TO START Sow seeds or plant seedlings 2 to 3 weeks after the last spring frost date. Grow bush types in hills 2 to 3 feet (0.61–0.91 m) apart in rows 3 to 5 feet (0.91–1.5 m) apart.

HARVEST Check squash vines every day once they start fruiting because squash grow rapidly—especially in hot temperatures. Summer squash tastes better and is more tender when eaten small. Picking produces more squash. Allowing fruits to ripen on the vine results in less production.

PESTS AND DISEASES Summer squash varieties appeal to many insects—borers, cucumber beetles, and squash bugs. One of the most destructive diseases for squash is bacterial wilt, which is carried by cucumber beetles. Watch for this insect and act swiftly. Control them with an insecticide approved for use on vegetables.

117 TAKE THESE TIPS TO THE GARDEN

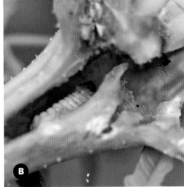

BLACK PLASTIC Around the base of plants, use black plastic or a thick layer of organic mulch (A).

PESTS Watch for evidence of pests. Squash vine borers burrow into the vines and eat from within (B).

SQUASH BLOSSOMS Pick squash blossoms and eat them—raw or cooked. Female blossoms produce squash fruit, so harvest the male blossoms to eat. Male blossoms have thinner stems than females and are the first flowers produced (C).

ADD A RAISED BED Even a small garden has room for a raised bed—the ideal venue for this prolific producer (D).

118
KNOW YOUR VARIETIES

'BLACK BEAUTY' This zucchini variety bears smooth, straight fruits on an open plant and is ready for picking in 60 days.

'EARLY PROLIFIC STRAIGHTNECK' An open-pollinated yellow squash with light cream–colored fruits. The neck end is thinner than the blossom end. It's ready to pick in 48 days.

'EARLY SUMMER CROOKNECK' An heirloom that has a bent neck and yellow fruits with bumpy skin. It's used like zucchini and is ready in 53 days.

'GOLD RUSH' This zucchini has golden-yellow, smooth, straight fruits—a colorful contrast to green zucchini—and is ready in 45 days.

'RAVEN HYBRID' This zucchini plant is a compact bush and produces dark green fruits in as few as 48 days from planting.

'SUNBURST' This pattypan variety is a deep golden-yellow, flat, and round summer squash with scalloped edges. It produces vigorously and is ready in 50 days.

It's good that so many recipes call for summer squash — it's the most enthusiastic producer in the garden. Choose squash that feel heavy for their size and have glossy skin.

119
TOSS SOME SQUASH ON THE GRILL

This grilled salad is simplicity itself—just slender slices of grilled zucchini and/or summer squash dressed with olive oil, lemon juice, fresh dill, and crushed red pepper, then accompanied by torn pieces of fresh mozzarella.

PREP: 10 minutes   GRILL: 6 minutes   MAKES: 4 servings

- 3 medium zucchini or summer squash, sliced lengthwise into ¼-inch (6 mm) planks
- 3 tablespoons extra-virgin olive oil
  Salt and ground black pepper
- 1 8-ounce (225-g) fresh mozzarella ball, pulled into large pieces
- 2 tablespoons coarsely snipped fresh dill
- ¼ teaspoon crushed red pepper
- 1 teaspoon lemon juice

STEP 1 On a baking sheet arrange the zucchini in a single layer. Drizzle with 1 tablespoon oil and sprinkle with salt and pepper.

STEP Grill zucchini directly over medium heat for 6 to 8 minutes or until tender, turning once.

STEP 3 On a serving platter arrange warm zucchini and mozzarella. Sprinkle with dill and crushed red pepper. Drizzle with lemon juice and the remaining 2 tablespoons oil.

EACH SERVING *265 cal, 22 g fat, 40 mg chol, 323 mg sodium, 3 g carb, 1 g fiber, 11 g pro*

120
FRITTER AROUND WITH ZUCCHINI

The key to getting the crispiest fritters is to press out as much water as possible from the shredded zucchini before combining it with the shredded potato. Lemon-caper mayo provides the finishing touch.

PREP: 35 minutes   COOK: 8 minutes   MAKES: 5 servings

8	ounces (225 g) zucchini, coarsely shredded
½	teaspoon salt
1	lemon
⅓	cup (75 g) mayonnaise
1	tablespoon capers, drained and coarsely chopped
1	teaspoon snipped fresh thyme
⅛	teaspoon ground black pepper
8	ounces (225 g) russet potatoes
½	cup (63 g) all-purpose flour
½	teaspoon baking powder
⅛	teaspoon cayenne pepper
1	egg, lightly beaten
2	tablespoons olive oil

STEP 1 Line a 15×10×1-inch (38×25×2.5-cm) baking pan with several layers of paper towels. Spread zucchini on paper towels; sprinkle with salt. Top with another layer of paper towels. Let stand for 15 minutes, pressing occasionally to release liquid.

STEP 2 Meanwhile, for caper mayonnaise, remove 1 teaspoon zest and 2 teaspoons juice from the lemon. In a bowl stir together lemon juice, mayonnaise, capers, thyme, and black pepper.

STEP 3 Transfer zucchini to a large bowl. Peel and finely shred the potatoes; add to the zucchini. Add the lemon zest, flour, baking powder, and cayenne pepper; toss to mix well. Add egg, stirring until combined.

STEP 4 In a large nonstick skillet heat 2 teaspoons of the oil over medium-high heat. Working in batches, drop batter by slightly rounded tablespoons into the hot skillet. Use a spatula to flatten into patties. Cook 4 to 5 minutes per side or until golden brown. (Keep fritters warm in 200°F/93°C oven while cooking additional batches.) Repeat with remaining batter, adding oil as needed. Serve fritters with caper mayonnaise.

EACH SERVING *249 cal, 18 g fat, 43 mg chol, 436 mg sodium, 18 g carb, 1 g fiber, 4 g pro*

BEANS

This crisp green vegetable is as diverse in the garden as on the plate. Dangling like pendants amid dark foliage, they are dark green, pale yellow, deep purple—even speckled. They range in size from thick pods to long slender pods. Plants range from 2 feet (61 cm) tall for bush types to pole types that may climb to 12 feet (3.7 m). Snap beans, or green beans, are easy to grow, bothered by few pests. If you choose pole types, they take little square footage in the garden. Even if you don't have a traditional vegetable garden, you can grow pole beans on fences or other upright support.

Beans can be eaten at various stages of growth. A bean (*Phaseolus vulgaris*) harvested when young, before seeds fully develop, is a snap bean. Once the seeds reach full size but pods have not turned brown, it's a shelling bean. After the pod dries and seeds mature, it's a dried bean.

Prepare beans in a variety of ways. Cook them whole, cut them crosswise or diagonally, or serve them French-cut (cut lengthwise). To preserve the natural sweetness of beans, don't cut them at all. Prepare them grilled, steamed, baked, or raw. And if you have a bumper crop, blanch extras to freeze. Use yellow, purple, and speckled beans raw in salads to showcase their brilliant colors. Once you cook them, they turn green.

121
PLANT, GROW & HARVEST

SITE Beans need sun and warm weather with well-drained soil.

BEDMATES Don't plant beans in the same place as other beans or peas. Rotate beds every year.

CARE Beans grow best when daytime temperatures are 70°F to 80°F (21–27°C). They can drop blossoms when temperatures go above 85°F (29°C). A frost kills beans, and plants may drop blossoms and pods if temperatures dip to 35°F (1.7°C).

HOW TO START Beans are among the easiest-to-grow vegetables. Sow seeds directly into the ground (after danger of frost has passed). For long and varied harvest, sow different varieties every 2 weeks.

HARVEST Pick every day to ensure plants keep producing. Harvest snap beans when pods are 6 to 8 inches (15–20 cm) long, 45 to 55 days after planting. Harvest bush beans when pods are ¼ inch (6 mm) in diameter. Harvest shelling beans once seeds reach full size, about 80 days after planting. Dried beans take 100 to 120 days to reach maturity. Harvest lima beans for shelling when the seeds reach full size and pods are plump. For dried lima beans, wait until pods turn brown.

PESTS AND DISEASES Not many insects or diseases go after beans. Handpick any beetles on plants. Also, crop rotation takes care of most diseases.

122 TAKE THESE TIPS TO THE GARDEN

PLANT Seeds should be planted every 4 inches (10 cm) in rows 2 feet (61 cm) apart for bush types. Plant seeds every 8 inches (20 cm) in rows 3 feet (91 cm) apart for pole types.

THIN Seedlings should be thinned to one every 4 to 8 inches (10–20 cm) (A).

POLE BEANS Because they grow vertically, pole beans need support. Train beans on trellises or fences or create rustic supports such as branches or tepees (B).

PLANT For a long harvest, plant bush beans at 2- to 3-week intervals throughout the season.

CUT To encourage branching, cut the terminal end off the top of pole beans.

WEED Pull weeds around the base of pole beans to keep them from growing up through the supports.

PICK Pods taste best when they are small and tender. Pinch or cut off the pods to avoid pulling the plant out of the ground.

123
KNOW YOUR POLE BEAN VARIETIES

'ROMANO' This plant forms vigorous vine and pods that remain stringless even when large.

'KENTUCKY BLUE' This variety produces round, 6- to 7-inch (15–18-cm), sweet-flavored pods. Approximately 60 days to maturity.

'KENTUCKY WONDER' Meaty pods that are stringless when young.

'BLUE LAKE' Good for eating fresh out of the garden. Approximately 64 days to maturity.

124
KNOW YOUR BUSH BEAN VARIETIES

'PURPLE QUEEN' A showy purple bean that turns green when cooked.

'ROSE' This variety offers marbled red and cream color. It's delicious for summer salads and soups.

'BLUE LAKE 274' This variety produces 6-inch (15-cm) green pods on bushy plants.

'DERBY' These plants resist disease well, and produce tender, 7-inch (18-cm) pods.

'JADE' This variety bears slender, deep green pods that remain tender and productive in the heat of summer.

'ROC D'OR' A yellow-pod snap bean that's also called wax bean. It bears 6-inch (15-cm) yellow pods 52 days after planting.

'ROYAL BURGUNDY' The purple pods of this variety turn green when cooked.

125
GET HOOKED ON 'FORDHOOK'

'FORDHOOK' Lima beans do well even in colder climates. They are ready to shell in 85 days or can be harvested in 95 to 100 days for dried butter beans.

126
TOSS GREEN BEANS IN A SUMMER SALAD

This "farmer's" salad is chock-full of ingredients that hit their stride in the peak of summer—corn, green beans, and tomatoes—dressed in a spicy jalapeño-cilantro dressing and topped with tangy Cotija cheese.

START TO FINISH: 45 minutes   **MAKES:** 10 servings

3	ears fresh sweet corn, husks and silks removed
1½	pounds (700 g) fresh green beans, trimmed
3	cups (413 g) grape tomatoes
½	small red onion, thinly sliced
1	cup (24 g) snipped fresh cilantro
½	cup (125 mL) olive oil
3	jalapeños, stemmed, seeded, and chopped*
¼	cup (25 g) chopped shallots
3	tablespoons cider vinegar
1½	teaspoon bottled minced roasted garlic
¼	teaspoon salt
½	cup (60 g) crumbled Cotija cheese

STEP 1 In a large pot cook corn in plenty of boiling salted water 5 to 7 minutes or until tender. Remove corn from pot. Add green beans to the boiling water; cook 3 to 4 minutes or just until crisp-tender. Rinse the beans in a colander with cold water, then drain well. Cut kernels from corn cobs.

STEP 2 In a large bowl combine corn kernels, green beans, tomatoes, and red onion. Toss gently to combine.

STEP 3 For dressing, in a food processor or blender combine the next seven ingredients (through salt). Cover and process or blend until nearly smooth. Drizzle dressing over vegetables; toss well to coat. Sprinkle with cheese. Serve immediately.

***TIP** Chile peppers contain oils that can irritate skin and eyes. Wear plastic or rubber gloves when working with them.

EACH SERVING *175 cal, 13 g fat, 5 mg chol, 71 mg sodium, 13 g carb, 3 g fiber, 4 g pro*

127
BLISTER GREEN BEANS

"Blistering" simply refers to cooking a food (usually a vegetable) at high heat until it gets beautifully browned and even charred in spots. This soy-glazed flank steak is served with spicy blistered green beans.

START TO FINISH: 35 minutes   MAKES: 4 servings

- 1   pound (450 g) fresh green beans
- 1   pound (450 g) beef flank steak
- 6   cloves garlic, minced
- 1   tablespoon grated fresh ginger
- 2   tablespoons soy sauce
- 1   teaspoon packed brown sugar
- 2   to 3 tablespoons peanut oil
- 4   green onions, white parts only, thinly sliced
- 2   tablespoons sweet rice wine (mirin)
- 1   teaspoon red chile paste (sambal oelek)
     Toasted sesame seeds (optional)
     Hot cooked rice (optional)

STEP 1 Trim green beans; set aside. Cut flank steak across the grain into thin slices; set aside. In a small bowl combine garlic and ginger; set aside. In another small bowl combine soy sauce and brown sugar; set aside.

STEP 2 In an extra-large skillet or wok heat 2 tablespoons of the oil over medium-high heat. Add green beans; cook and stir 7 to 8 minutes or until beans are blistered and brown in spots. Transfer beans to paper towels to drain. If necessary, add the remaining 1 tablespoon oil to skillet.

STEP 3 Add garlic-ginger mixture to the skillet; cook and stir 30 seconds. Add half the beef strips to skillet. Cook and stir about

3 minutes or until beef browns. Using a slotted spoon, transfer beef to a medium bowl. Repeat to cook remaining beef. Return all beef to skillet. Stir in green onions, rice wine, chile paste, and soy sauce-sugar mixture. Cook and stir for 1 minute; add beans. Cook and

stir 2 minutes more or until green beans are heated through.

STEP 4 If desired, sprinkle with sesame seeds and serve with hot cooked rice if desired.

EACH SERVING *312 cal, 16 g fat, 53 mg chol, 672 mg sodium, 15 g carb, 4 g fiber, 28 g pro*

CUCUMBERS

Cucumbers are easy to grow and so prolific. Just one plant produces armloads of crunchy, refreshing fruits. Cucumbers are grouped as slicers or picklers. All slicers are long and thin and are best eaten fresh. Picklers, which are shorter with more pronounced spines or bumps on their skin, are most often preserved as pickles but can be eaten fresh too. Bush varieties produce vines only several feet long and are suited to growing in containers, on trellises, and along fences for efficient use of space. Keep cucumbers watered well to avoid moisture stress, which leads to bitterness.

Cucumbers (*Cucumis sativus*) include several varieties. The best pickling cucumbers, Kirby cucumbers, are small, just a few to several inches long, and easily pack into jars. They have firm flesh with few seeds and the skin is thin, which allows brine to penetrate.

Regular, larger garden cucumbers don't work as well for pickling. You can use supermarket English cucumbers, which are long, slender, and wrapped in plastic (though they are prohibitively expensive for large canning projects). Don't use the common waxed cucumber sold at supermarkets; the coating keeps the cucumber fresh longer but interferes with its ability to absorb brine. Test for waxy coating by scraping a thumbnail along the cucumber.

128
PLANT, GROW & HARVEST

SITE Plant cucumbers in a sunny spot with about 6 feet (1.8 m) to spread. In a small garden grow bush varieties, which produce short vines; they are suited to growing in containers and on trellises.

BEDMATES Cucumbers have the same growing conditions as beans. Plant cucumbers beneath corn plants to crawl up the stalks.

CARE Keep cucumbers watered well; if they get too dry they become bitter. Use black or brown plastic mulch to discourage weeds and help plants develop in warm, moist soil to improve production.

HOW TO START Sow seeds in the garden after the soil has warmed. Or buy cucumber seedlings and transplant them in the garden after the danger of frost has passed.

HARVEST Once cucumber fruits set, they develop quickly. Harvest every few days to prevent oversize fruits, which can be bitter and have too many seeds.

PESTS AND DISEASES Cucumbers are bugged by a few pests: cucumber beetles, aphids, and spider mites. Cucumber beetles cause the most damage, especially to seedlings. Deter them by placing a floating row cover over emerging seedlings to keep moths from laying eggs. Remove the cover when plants flower so they can then be pollinated.

129 TAKE THESE TIPS TO THE GARDEN

SOW Seeds can be planted outdoors after soil has warmed in spring. Plant groups of 5 or 6 seeds ½ inch (12 mm) deep in rows 6 feet (1.8 m) apart (A).

USE Cover plants with fabric to deter cucumber beetles (B).

LOOK Be alert for cucumber beetles on flowers and leaves; they cause damage to blooms and seedlings by spreading wilt disease. Pick them off and destroy (C).

GROW Trellises or fences make efficient use of space for growing cucumbers (D).

Cucumbers are more than 90 percent water. Even at room temperature, all of that moisture makes the flesh feel cool and refreshing.

130 KNOW YOUR VARIETIES

'BUSH PICKLE' This compact plant bears 5-inch- (13-cm-) long fruits in just 45 days. It adapts well to container culture.

'GREEN FINGERS' This variety features tender, smooth, finger-size fruits with no bitterness. It has a small seed cavity and is highly flavorful. It's ready in 60 days.

'LEMON' An heirloom that bears 2- to 3-inch- (5–8-cm-) round yellow fruits within 60 days that can be used for pickling or slicing.

'MARKETER' This variety is an old-time favorite and the 1943 All America Selections winner. Its 8-inch- (20-cm-) long burpless fruits mature in just 45 days.

'SALAD BUSH HYBRID' An 8-inch- (20-cm-) long slicer that grows on a compact plant. Fruits are ready to harvest in 57 days.

'SWEET SUCCESS' This variety develops fruits without pollination for extra yields. It's also disease-resistant and burpless, which means it's nearly seedless and easier on the tummy. It's ready for picking in 54 days.

'TASTY JADE HYBRID' A vigorous high yielder that produces 1-foot- (30-cm-) long fruits in 54 days. The plant must be trellised.

131
SIP SOME CUCUMBER SANGRIA

This refreshing sangria made with cucumber, honeydew melon, lime, and just a little bit of honey is lighter and crisper than most sangrias that use red wine as a base.

PREP: 20 minutes   CHILL: 2 hours   MAKES: 8 servings

1	small honeydew melon
1	seedless cucumber, thinly sliced
1	lime, thinly sliced
12	fresh mint leaves
¼	cup (50 mL) lime juice
¼	cup (50 mL) honey
1	750-mL bottle Sauvignon blanc or other semi-dry white wine, chilled
1	1-L bottle carbonated water, chilled
	Fresh mint sprigs and/or leaves (optional)

STEP 1 Cut the melon in half; remove and discard seeds and rind. Cut melon into thin slices. In a large pitcher combine melon, cucumber, lime slices, and the 12 mint leaves. In a small bowl stir together lime juice and honey until combined; pour over melon mixture. Add wine, stirring gently. Cover and chill at least 2 hours.

STEP 2 To serve, stir in carbonated water. Ladle or pour into glasses. If desired, garnish with additional mint.

EACH SERVING *147 cal, 1 g fat, 0 mg chol, 18 mg sodium, 21 g carb, 1 g fiber, 1 g pro*

132
ENJOY CRUNCH TIME WITH CUCUMBERS

This salad is made with two of summer's favorite veggies—cucumber and radishes. Just slice and toss with salt, vinegar, olive oil, and lime juice. Right before serving, toss the peppery radish tops into the salad.

PREP: 25 minutes   STAND: 1 hour   MAKES: 8 servings

12	radishes with green tops
1	seedless English cucumber, washed and cut thinly in rounds
½	teaspoon kosher salt
½	cup (125 mL) rice vinegar
2	tablespoons extra-virgin olive oil
2	tablespoons fresh lime juice

STEP 1 Wash green radish tops; thinly slice and set aside. Thinly slice radish bulbs.

STEP 2 In a large bowl toss the radish and cucumber slices with salt. Toss with vinegar, oil, and lime juice. Let stand at room temperature for 1 hour. Just before serving, fold radish tops into salad.

EACH SERVING *45 cal, 3 g fat, 0 mg chol, 127 mg sodium, 2 g carb, 0 g fiber, 0 g pro*

STRAWBERRIES

With their low-growing nature and bright green foliage, strawberries are an attractive groundcover that produces a sweet crop. Many gardeners include strawberries as ornamentals in flowerbeds. Tucked in a container or hanging basket, strawberries offer snacks to anyone who walks across the patio. The classic strawberry pot holds several plants in one container.

Three types of strawberries are categorized by when they bear and how they grow: June-bearing, everbearing, and day-neutral. For big, juicy berries, plant June-bearing plants. These spring bearers pump out abundant fruit for just a few weeks. For a long harvest season, plant a mix of early, midseason, and late varieties to prolong the sweet feast for more than the 2- to 3-week span that June-bearing plants produce. This strawberry spreads better than other types. Because it sends out lots of runners, it's the best choice for a bed or large planting as the spread becomes dense and more productive.

Everbearing strawberries yield lightly all summer long—producing two or three major harvests during spring, summer, and fall. These plants do not produce many runners. Day-neutral strawberries also produce fruit throughout the season and produce few runners. Both everbearing and day-neutral strawberries are good choices for small-space gardens.

133
PLANT, GROW & HARVEST

SITE Choose a warm, sunny location with good drainage. If you have heavy soil, plant strawberries in raised beds. Space plants 18 to 24 inches (46–61 cm) apart in rows 2 to 4 feet (0.61–1.2 m) apart. Day-neutral types can be planted closer together.

BEDMATES Do not plant strawberries anywhere members of the Solanaceae crops, berries, melons, or roses have been planted.

CARE Remove any runners after first planting strawberries. In a few years plants will have multiple crowns and you can let runners develop to replace the older plants. Apply a balanced water-soluble plant food as buds develop. After harvest, mow the leaves close to the ground. Mulch in winter.

HOW TO START Grow from runners.

HARVEST Begin harvesting most types the year after planting, about 14 months from planting in cooler climates and 9 months in warmer zones. The highest yields will come from the youngest plants.

PESTS AND DISEASES Purchase varieties resistant to disease and plants guaranteed to be disease-free. Strawberries are susceptible to botrytis fruit rot, leaf spot, and leaf scorch. All can be controlled with adequate drainage, good bed maintenance, and fungicide if needed. Aphids and spider mites can be washed off by hard rains.

134 TAKE THESE TIPS TO THE GARDEN

PLANT Strawberries like a sunny spot with well-drained soil. Set the plant in the hole and fill in around the roots so the soil just covers the top of the roots (A).

GROW Strawberries do well in containers. A hanging basket also works well, or use a strawberry pot; two or three plants fill the top, and runners can fill the lower openings (B).

PROTECT In early spring, protect strawberry plants against frost. Use row covers to protect from temperatures as low as −25°F (−31°C) (C).

REMOVE Pinch off blossoms on strawberries the first year to promote root and runner development (and a larger crop of berries the following year) (D).

Strawberries are ripe when they are full color — regardless of size. They overripen quickly, so pick often.

135 KNOW YOUR VARIETIES

'RUGEN' This alpine strawberry bears small white flowers followed by tiny berries all summer. Popular as an edging plant, it forms a tidy clump.

'TRISTAR' An everbearing strawberry that produces from June until the first frost. It is excellent eaten fresh or frozen.

'STRAWBERRY FESTIVAL' A firm, long-lasting berry that's delicious in fruit salads.

'CAMINO REAL' A large strawberry well suited for dipping in chocolate.

'CAMAROSA' BERRY This variety is red all the way through. It's a sweet berry that's good for cakes and shortcake.

'ALLSTAR' Known for exceptionally large berries, this June-bearer has good flavor and produces late in the month.

'EARLIGLOW' An early producer with excellent flavor. It has modest yields, and berry size decreases as the season progresses.

'ALBION' A large supersweet berry that grows best in cold climates.

136
SWEETEN A SALAD WITH STRAWBERRIES

Peppery arugula provides the perfect contrast to the sweetness of summer-ripe strawberries in this gorgeous salad. Cheese crisps ("fricos" in Italian) made from Manchego cheese offer a savory taste.

PREP: 15 minutes   COOK: 9 minutes   MAKES: 6 servings

- 1 cup (115 g) shredded Manchego cheese, shredded
- 3 tablespoons olive oil
- 3 tablespoons balsamic vinegar
- ¼ teaspoon kosher salt
- ¼ teaspoon freshly ground black pepper
- 3 cups (432 g) strawberries, halved and/or quartered
- 4 cups (80 g) baby arugula

STEP 1 For fricos, heat a medium nonstick skillet over medium heat. Sprinkle one-third of the cheese over the bottom of the skillet, shaking the skillet so cheese is in an even layer. Cook 2 to 3 minutes or until cheese browns around the edges. Remove skillet from heat for 30 to 40 seconds or until cheese is set. Using a spatula and fork, carefully turn frico over, return to heat, and cook 1 to 2 minutes more or until underside is golden. Slide frico out of pan onto a wire rack. Repeat with the remaining cheese to make 3 fricos.

STEP 2 For salad, in a large bowl combine oil, balsamic vinegar, salt, and pepper. Add strawberries and arugula; toss to coat. Transfer salad to 6 serving plates or a large platter.

STEP 3 Break fricos into pieces and serve with salad.

EACH SERVING *165 cal, 13 g fat, 17 mg chol, 192 mg sodium, 8 g carb, 2 g fiber, 6 g pro*

137
MAKE A STRAWBERRY MERINGUE

Pavlova—a Russian dessert named for a prima ballerina—is a crisp meringue shell filled with fresh seasonal fruit.

PREP: 40 minutes **STAND:** 1 hour 50 minutes **BAKE:** 1 hour 30 minutes at 250°F (120°C) **MAKES:** 8 servings

6	egg whites
	Pinch salt
	Pinch cream of tartar
1½	cups (300 g) sugar
1	teaspoon lemon juice
½	teaspoon vanilla
2½	teaspoons cornstarch
4	cups (576 g) strawberries
2	tablespoons sugar
10	mint leaves, torn
1½	cups (375 mL) heavy cream
½	cup (125 mL) crème fraîche

STEP 1 Allow egg whites to stand at room temperature for 30 minutes. Line a baking sheet with parchment paper. Draw a 9-inch (23-cm) circle on the paper; invert so circle is on reverse side.

STEP 2 Preheat oven to 250°F (120°C). For meringue, in a bowl beat egg whites, salt, and cream of tartar with a mixer on medium until soft peaks form (tips curl). Add the 1½ cups (300 g) sugar, 1 tablespoon at a time, beating on high until stiff peaks form (tips stand straight). Beat in lemon juice and vanilla. Sift cornstarch over egg whites; gently fold.

STEP 3 Spread meringue over circle on paper, building up edges slightly to form a shell. Bake 1½ hours (do not open door). Turn off oven; let meringue dry in oven with door closed for 1 hour.

STEP 4 For filling, 20 minutes before serving, clean, hull, and slice the strawberries; place in a large bowl. Toss berries with the 2 tablespoons sugar. Stir mint into strawberries. Let stand 20 minutes.

STEP 5 Meanwhile, in a large bowl beat the cream and crème fraîche with a mixer on medium until soft peaks form (tips curl).

STEP 6 Place meringue shell on a large platter. Spread the cream into the meringue shell, top with strawberries. Serve immediately.

EACH SERVING *404 cal, 22 g fat, 82 mg chol, 83 mg sodium, 49 g carb, 1 g fiber, 4 g pro*

RASPBERRIES

Enjoy these berries in so many colors. Red, yellow, purple, or black—you may want to carve out a little room for each. Raspberries prefer sunny spots, although they frequently grow wild in shaded areas. Black raspberries tolerate the most heat.

There are two types of raspberries—summer-bearers and ever-bearers—both with their own specific requirements for growing. Summer bearers produce one crop in the summer and plants should be pruned in the fall. Ever-bearers produce two crops, one mid-summer and one in the fall. Mow ever-bearers to the ground after the last harvest. Plant more than one variety so you can savor various ripening times and harvests. Red and yellow fruits grow one or two crops on stiff, arching canes. Black and purple fruits grow one crop on trailing canes that require trellising.

Raspberries (*Rubus idaeus*) are a special treat and they taste best picked fresh—this soft fruit does not ship well. Raspberries are fruit-producing powerhouses. Mature red raspberry plants can produce from 1 to 2 pounds (0.5–1 kg) of fruit; purple and black raspberries are even more prolific. This plump, seedy fruit grows wild—sown, in part, by birds that eat berries and deposit seeds in their droppings. Wild raspberries are smaller than cultivated raspberries.

138
PLANT, GROW & HARVEST

SITE Plant raspberries where they will receive full sun and good drainage. In water-retaining clay soils, mound soil into raised beds to keep the canes from developing root rot. Plants are healthier with good ventilation.

BEDMATES Don't plant raspberries in garden beds where tomatoes, potatoes, eggplants, or peppers have recently grown.

CARE Apply fertilizers in early spring and again in late spring for fall-bearing plants. In spring remove mature canes and thin new growth. Support on wires stretched between posts. Prune out the current season's fruiting canes after harvesting. Raspberries will spread rapidly by underground runners if not kept in check. Prune the fruiting canes in fall. Berries will form on new canes.

HOW TO START Grow raspberries from root or stem cuttings. Buy bare-root, virus-free plants in early spring. Plant in rows 2 to 4 feet (0.61–1.2 m) apart. Start raspberries from new suckers.

HARVEST Raspberries bear a small crop the second year after planting and a full crop the third year. They are productive for 5 to 8 years.

PESTS AND DISEASES A number of fungal diseases attack plants. Plant virus-free nursery stock. Insect pests include raspberry cane borer and Japanese beetles, which feed on fruit and leaves.

139 TAKE THESE TIPS TO THE GARDEN

PRUNE Each year in early spring, use pruning shears to cut back canes. Pruning raspberries makes healthy, productive plants (A).

PINCH Remove the tips of purple and black raspberry canes in summer to promote branching (B).

PLANT In spring, plant canes in a row with 2 to 4 feet (0.61–1.2 m) between plants.

DIVIDE/REPLANT In spring or fall, divide and replant canes to increase patch size. Use a spade to chop divisions.

FERTILIZE Give raspberries a boost at planting time by adding compost or a 10-10-10 fertilizer to the soil.

KEEP BIRDS AWAY If birds dip into the harvest, drape netting (sold at garden centers) over the canes. Lift the net to pick berries.

MAINTAIN Keep canes off the ground so berries are easy to pick and are unmarred.

141
EXPAND YOUR RASPBERRY KNOWLEDGE

Raspberries almost melt in your mouth because of their soft texture and sweet taste. Each raspberry consists of about 100 individual tiny fruits, called drupelets, filled with one seed, arranged in the shape of a helmet around a centrally positioned small stem. When ripe raspberries are harvested from the plant, the stem remains on the mother plant, leaving a hole in the top of the fruit.

140
KNOW YOUR RASPBERRY VARIETIES

'BRISTOL' All-purpose raspberry that bears large, firm, glossy black berries for several weeks in summer. Upright canes don't require staking. Pick in early July.

'JEWEL' This black raspberry is a productive plant ands bears black-purple berries in early July. Reliable, hardy, and flavorful.

'FALL GOLD' This ever-bearer variety produces sweet, gold berries and two crops—one in early summer and a second in fall. It's a good choice for cooler climates.

'ROYALTY' A hardy, vigorous variety that is resistant to insects and disease. This plant bears large, sweet, purple fruit that bursts with flavor. Easy to grow. Harvest in July.

'CANBY' This variety produces large firm red berries in midseason. Plants are semi-thornless and do best in well-drained soils in the warmer and temperate climates.

'WILLAMETTE' The berries of this plant are red, large, round, and firm and they ripen midseason. This vigorous plant is a popular commercial variety and good for warmer climates.

'HERITAGE' This red raspberry variety bears medium-size sweet, dark red berries in early summer (June) and again in autumn (September). Canes are upright and don't require support. Cold-hardy and does well in poor soils.

'MEEKER' This variety produces bright red berries on strong, disease-resistant plants.

'REVEILLE' Bred for early fruiting, this variety has large, red, sweet-tasting berries. Plants are vigorous and productive.

'TITAN' This variety produces large, luscious, red fruits. The plants require well-drained, light soil.

142
FREEZE YOUR RASPBERRY ASSETS

Plan well ahead to serve this refreshing raspberry sorbet. It doesn't take long at all to prep, but it has to freeze in two different stages for a total of 10 hours.

PREP: 20 minutes **CHILL:** 1 hour **FREEZE:** 10 hours **STAND:** 5 minutes **MAKES:** 9 servings

1   cup (200 g) sugar
1   cup (250 mL) water
2   tablespoons lemon juice
3   cups (375 g) fresh raspberries
2   tablespoons orange juice

STEP 1 For syrup, in a medium saucepan heat and stir sugar and the water over medium heat just until simmering, stirring to dissolve sugar. Remove from heat; stir in lemon juice. Transfer to a medium bowl; cover and chill completely.

STEP 2 Place raspberries and orange juice in a food processor or blender. Cover and process or blend until smooth. Press puree through a fine-mesh sieve; discard seeds. Stir puree into chilled syrup.

STEP 3 Spread raspberry mixture in a 2-quart (2 L) square baking dish. Cover and freeze about 4 hours or until firm. Break up mixture with a fork; place in food processor or blender, half at a time if necessary. Cover and process or blend for 30 to 60 seconds or until smooth and lightened in color. Spoon sorbet back into the dish; cover and freeze 6 to 8 hours more or until firm. To serve, let stand at room temperature for 5 minutes before scooping.

EACH SERVING *110 cal, 0 fat, 0 mg chol, 1 mg sodium, 28 g carb, 3 g fiber, 1 g pro*

143
MAKE A BERRY-TOPPED BREAKFAST BOWL

Use a vegetable peeler to make ribbons of melon that are tossed with a licoricey anise syrup and topped with fresh raspberries, yogurt, and granola.

PREP: 40 minutes   CHILL: 1 hour   MAKES: 8 servings

- 2   cups (475 mL) orange juice
- ¼   cup (50 mL) honey
- 1   teaspoon anise seeds
- ¼   to ½ teaspoon cracked pink or green peppercorns
- 1   ripe cantaloupe and/or honeydew melon, halved, seeded, and peeled
- 2   teaspoons snipped fresh mint
- 1½   cups (188 g) fresh red raspberries
- 1   recipe poppy seed yogurt (optional)
- 1   cup (122 g) granola (optional)
- 8   mint sprigs

STEP 1 For anise syrup, in a medium saucepan combine orange juice, honey, anise seeds, and peppercorns. Bring to boiling; reduce heat. Simmer, uncovered, 10 to 15 minutes or until slightly syrupy. Remove from heat; let cool. Cover and chill at least 30 minutes or up to 24 hours.

STEP 2 For melon ribbons, draw a vegetable peeler across each melon half (or use a mandoline). Place melon in a large bowl. Stir the 2 teaspoons mint into anise syrup. Add anise syrup to melon ribbons; gently toss to coat. Cover; chill at least 30 minutes or up to 24 hours.

STEP 3 To make the poppy seed yogurt (optional), in a bowl stir together one 7-ounce (200-g) carton plain Greek yogurt, ½ teaspoon orange zest, and ½ teaspoon poppy seeds. Cover and chill up to 4 hours.

STEP 4 To serve, using a slotted spoon, divide melon among 8 dessert dishes. Sprinkle with raspberries. Drizzle with some of the anise syrup remaining in bowl. If desired, top with poppy seed yogurt and sprinkle with granola. Garnish with mint sprigs.

EACH SERVING *92 cal, 0 fat, 0 mg chol, 12 mg sodium, 23 g carb, 2 g fiber, 1 g pro*

CHERRIES

In the early spring, cherry trees burst into a cloud of crepe-paper petaled bloom. Cherries are either sweet or sour. Sweet cherries, such as 'Bing' and the decadently sweet 'Rainier,' can be eaten right off the tree. Their tart cousins, the sour cherry (also called tart cherries), include 'Nanking' and 'Montmorency' and are excellent choices for baking as long as a bit of sugar is added to sweeten them.

Cherry trees range in size from standard to semidwarf and dwarf. Space standard cherry trees 25 to 50 feet (7.6–15 m) apart, semidwarfs 15 to 25 feet (4.6–7.6 m) apart, and dwarfs 8 to 12 feet (2.5–3.7 m) apart. If you plant an orchard of cherry trees, choose small trees that are easy to harvest.

With smooth-skinned, globular flesh and a big pit, cherries are an exclusive fruit to the northern hemisphere. There are many cherry varieties, including wild species, that grow native in North America, Europe, and Asia. Sweet and sour cherries are cousins in the *Prunus* genus. The majority of sweet cherries are *Prunus avium*. The sour cherry is *Prunus cerasus*.

Sour cherries begin to bear 3 to 4 years after planting. Fruits ripen about 60 days after bloom, from late May to mid-June. Sweet cherries begin producing heavy yields in their fifth year and bear fruit in July. Store ripe cherries up to a week in the refrigerator.

144
PLANT, GROW & HARVEST

SITE Cherries need a sunny location and fertile, well-drained soil. Bush-type cherries can tolerate heavy and alkaline soils. Cherries thrive where winters and summers are mild.

BEDMATES Sweet cherries require a pollinator. Plant two varieties. Sour or pie cherries are self-fertile—only one plant is necessary for fruit to set.

CARE Prune sour cherry trees to form an open or vase shape. Prune sweet cherry trees to help form a central leader, meaning branches grow only from the tree's center. After planting, clip off side branches but leave the leader.

HOW TO START Purchase cherry trees as bare-root or container-grown plants.

HARVEST Sour cherries begin to bear 3 to 4 years after planting. Fruits ripen about 60 days after flowers bloom. Harvest sour cherries from late May through mid-June. Sweet cherries produce heavy yields in their fifth year. Harvest fruits in July.

PESTS AND DISEASES Cherry trees are susceptible to molds, including fusarium wilt, which is more prevalent in hot and humid conditions. Other common problems include plum curculio, brown rot, fruit flies, leaf spot, and bacterial canker.

145 TAKE THESE TIPS TO THE GARDEN

PLANT To plant a container-grown cherry tree, dig a hole the same depth as the length of the roots (about the same depth the container but twice as wide) in a sunny location. Firm the soil around the roots to eliminate air pockets in the soil (A).

ADD Drape protective netting to keep birds from eating cherries (B).

CLIP After you plant, clip off side branches of sweet cherries—but leave the leader (C).

146
KNOW YOUR SOUR CHERRY VARIETIES

'ENGLISH MORELLO' This late-ripening variety produces tart dark red to nearly black fruit.

'MONTMORENCY' A medium to large sour cherry tree. It produces masses of large red fruit with yellow flesh.

'NORTHSTAR' This variety is a heavy producer. Big harvests start in mid-June. 'Northstar' is hardy and disease-resistant.

'METEOR' A 10-foot (3-m) sour cherry tree that bears bright red fruit with yellow flesh.

147
KNOW YOUR SWEET CHERRY VARIETIES

'BING' This variety is the standard for sweet black cherries—and for eating out of hand. The deep mahogany-color fruit is firm, juicy, and generous in size. The large spreading tree yields big crops. Use 'Sam,' 'Van,' or 'Black Tartarian' as a pollenizer (not 'Royal Ann' or 'Lambert').

'ROYAL ANN' The standard for blushed yellow cherries. Trees bears large, firm, juicy fruit excellent for eating fresh or canning and preserves. The very large tree spreads with age. 'Royal Ann' is the cherry used to make maraschino cherries. Use 'Corum,' 'Windsor,' or 'Hedelfingen' as a pollenizer (not 'Bing' or 'Lambert').

'RAINIER' This variety features medium to large fruit with yellow skin that has a deep red blush. The sweet, firm, fine fruit has delicious yellow flesh. 'Rainier' ripens midseason.

'STELLA' A sweet cherry with sizable plump dark red fruit. The 25-foot (7.6-m) tree grows especially well in warmer climates 'Stella' is self-pollinating; you need only one tree.

148
MAKE A BROWNIE BETTER WITH CHERRIES

Cherries and chocolate are natural companions (think chocolate-covered cherries). Here, brandied cherries top rich and fudgy homemade brownies for a dessert that can be fancy or casual.

PREP: 25 minutes   BAKE: 25 minutes at 325°F (160°C)   COOL: 45 minutes   MAKES: 4 servings

⅔   cup (133 g) sugar

½   cup (125 mL) brandy

1   cup (155 g) fresh sweet cherries, stemmed, pitted, and halved
    Unsweetened cocoa powder

½   cup (115 g) butter

1   cup (200 g) sugar

¾   cup (75 g) unsweetened cocoa powder

1   teaspoon vanilla

½   teaspoon salt

2   eggs

⅓   cup (42 g) all-purpose flour
    Vanilla ice cream (optional)

STEP 1 For brandied cherries, in a small saucepan combine the ⅔ cup (133 g) sugar and the brandy. Bring to boiling; add cherries. Reduce heat; simmer, uncovered for 3 minutes. Remove from heat; let cool.

STEP 2 Preheat oven to 325°F (160°C). Grease an 8×8-inch (20×20-cm) baking pan. Line pan with foil, extending the foil 1 inch (2.5 cm) beyond pan edges. Grease the foil; sprinkle with cocoa powder.

STEP 3 In a small saucepan melt butter over low heat. Transfer melted butter to a bowl. Add the 1 cup (200 g) sugar, and the cocoa powder, vanilla, and salt. Stir until cocoa powder is completely incorporated. Add eggs, one at a time, beating with a spoon just

until combined. Add flour; stir just until combined. Spread batter in the prepared pan.

STEP 4 Bake 25 minutes or until edges start to pull away from sides of pan. Cool 45 minutes. Use foil to lift uncut brownies from pan. Cut warm brownies into

16 squares. Place 1 brownie in each of 4 shallow dishes. Top with brandied cherries. If desired, serve with ice cream.

EACH SERVING *379 cal, 7 g fat, 39 mg chol, 134 mg sodium, 66 g carb, 2 g fiber, 2 g pro*

149
SHERRY YOUR CHERRIES

The flavor of sherry enhances this crisp made with fresh and dried cherries. Pit cherries by pushing the narrow end of a chopstick through the stem end of each cherry; for high volume, a cherry pitter is a wise investment.

PREP: 25 minutes STAND: 30 minutes BAKE: 50 minutes at 375°F (190°C) MAKES: 6 servings

½ cup (57 g) dried tart red cherries

⅓ cup (75 mL) dry sherry or port wine

4 cups (565 g) fresh pitted tart red cherries

½ cup (100 g) granulated sugar

1 tablespoon all-purpose flour

1 teaspoon orange zest

¼ cup (50 mL) orange juice

¾ cup (94 g) all-purpose flour

½ cup (45 g) regular rolled oats

½ cup (99 g) packed brown sugar

½ teaspoon salt

½ teaspoon vanilla

⅓ cup (77 g) cold butter, cut up

STEP 1 In a small bowl soak the dried cherries in sherry for 30 minutes. If using frozen cherries, thaw for 30 to 45 minutes or until partially thawed. Meanwhile, lightly grease a 1½-quart (1½-L) baking dish or deep-dish pie plate; set aside.

STEP 2 Preheat oven to 375°F (190°C). In a medium bowl combine fresh cherries, granulated sugar, flour, orange zest, and orange juice. Stir in dried cherries with sherry. Pour cherry filling into prepared dish.

STEP 3 For topping, in a large bowl combine the ¾ cup (94 g) flour, the oats, brown sugar, and salt. Sprinkle with vanilla. Using a pastry blender, cut in butter until mixture resembles coarse crumbs. Sprinkle topping over filling.

STEP 4 Bake 50 minutes or until filling is bubbly over entire surface and topping is golden brown. Serve warm.

EACH SERVING *427 cal, 11 g fat, 27 mg chol, 295 mg sodium, 78 g carb, 4 g fiber, 4 g pro*

BLUEBERRIES

Blueberries are one of the only natural foods that are truly blue. Small, dark, sweet, and juicy, the blueberry is fairly easy to grow and a treat to eat right off the bush. Blueberries are key players in recipes, where they add color and sweetness to muffins, turnovers, and pancakes. Blueberry pies are simply divine. Juicy and plump, blueberries are also extremely perishable. Store them unwashed in the refrigerator up to 1 week. To enjoy fresh sweetness later in the season, rinse and dry berries and freeze them in single layers for long-term storage.

Although you may think of blueberries as being a cool climate fruit, warmer climates also grow this berry-producing shrub. There are blueberry varieties that are best suited for each climate. Certain varieties need a specific length of time in dormancy—in temperatures below 45°F (7°C) for fruit to set. Blueberries that fall into the "high chill" category need cooler winters to thrive. In warmer climates, a "low chill" variety will do best. The most commonly raised blueberry is the highbush blueberry, which grows about 4 to 7 feet (1.2–2 m) tall. Lowbush blueberries grow just 1 foot (30 cm) tall and spread by underground stems to form a dense mat. Blueberries can also be grown in containers—choose compact varieties such as 'TopHat' or 'Sunshine Blue Dwarf.'

150
PLANT, GROW & HARVEST

SITE Like most fruits, blueberries do best in full sun and prefer moist, well-drained soil that's rich in organic matter. Blueberries need soil with an acidic pH— ideally between 4.5 and 5.5. For neutral or alkaline soil, amend it with soil sulfur before planting.

BEDMATES Most blueberries need another variety nearby in order to bear lots of fruit. Plant at least two varieties of the same type.

CARE In acidic soil, most blueberries are low-maintenance. Remove all the flowers or fruits the first year planted. After planting, spread a 3-inch (8-cm) layer of mulch over the soil around the blueberries, leaving a gap of 1 or 2 inches (2.5–5 cm) at the stem. Water blueberries in times of drought, but don't let the soil stay soggy. Roots are very sensitive; fertilize at one-half or one-quarter the recommended rate.

HOW TO START Buy blueberry plants in bare-root or container-grown forms.

HARVEST Blueberries are ready to pick 2 to 4 months after flowering, from July to September.

PESTS AND DISEASES Birds, deer, and raccoons feast on blueberries, so protect crops with netting or fencing. Phomopsis canker, root rot, mummyberry, and twig blight can all affect blueberries. Japanese beetles are also a common pest.

151 TAKE THESE TIPS TO THE GARDEN

TASTY Pretty blue fruits and colorful red fall foliage make blueberries an outstanding addition to the landscape. Plant blueberries in mixed shrub borders and perennial beds for structure and interest as well as fruit production.

AMEND Before planting, check the pH of the soil, and, if needed, amend by forking in ammonium sulfate (A).

SET Plant bare-root stock at the same depth it was grown in the nursery, then cut back the plants by half to remove buds (B).

PLANT Blueberries should be planted in the spring in cooler climates and late fall in warmer climates.

GROW When soil isn't appropriate for blueberries (or space is limited), grow them in containers. Choose big containers—at least 36 inches (90 cm) in diameter if you live in a cold climate—and fill them with acidic potting mix. Water them so the soil stays moist but not wet.

152
EXPAND YOUR BLUEBERRY KNOWLEDGE

The blueberry has a bell-shape flower that can be white, pink, or red. Fruit changes color from greenish to reddish to dark purple when it ripens. Flowers contain both male (stamen) and female (pistil) reproductive organs. Honey bees and bumblebees are the main pollinators of blueberries.

153
KNOW YOUR VARIETIES

NORTHERN HIGHBUSH A popular North American species of blueberry that produces large berries. There are more than 100 named varieties. Common varieties include 'Bluecrop,' 'Earliblue,' and 'Jersey.'

SOUTHERN HIGHBUSH This variety is specifically hybridized for superior fruit, soil adaptability, and heat tolerance. They don't need as much winter cold to bear well, yet produce large flavorful fruits. Some plants are self-pollinating but the berries will be larger if two varieties are planted together. Popular varieties include 'Oneal,' 'Ozarkblue,' and 'Legacy.'

RABBITEYE Grown best in areas that have acidic soils, rabbiteye plants have few serious pests and low nutritional requirements. The harvest season is May through July in most locations. Top rabbiteye varieties include 'Premier' and 'Powderblue.'

LOWBUSH This variety is short in stature. Because they spread primarily by rhizomes, a mature planting can form a dense ground cover. Profuse white blooms yield small light blue fruit with an intense, sweet, and tangy blueberry flavor. Annual pruning is not necessary, but they respond well if two-thirds of the growth is cut back every second or third year in late winter.

154
FUEL UP WITH BLUEBERRY-STUDDED SALAD

With farro, spinach, and blueberries, this could rightfully be called a superfood salad. But just because it's healthful doesn't mean it's not delicious. Roasted pistachios add crunch; goat cheese adds a tart, creamy touch.

START TO FINISH: 45 minutes MAKES: 10 servings

1	tablespoon extra-virgin olive oil
3	shallots, finely chopped
2	cups (400 g) pearled farro
4	cups (1 L) reduced-sodium chicken broth
1	lemon
½	cup (125 mL) extra-virgin olive oil
1	tablespoon snipped fresh oregano
½	teaspoon kosher salt
¼	teaspoon cracked black pepper
4	cups (120 g) baby spinach leaves
2	cups (300 g) blueberries
1	fennel bulb, trimmed, halved, cored, and very thinly sliced
1	bunch green onions, thinly sliced
1	cup (123 g) roasted, salted pistachios, coarsely chopped
8	ounces (225 g) goat cheese, crumbled

STEP 1 In a large saucepan heat 1 tablespoon olive oil over medium heat. Add 2 of the shallots; cook and stir until translucent. Add farro; cook and stir 1 minute more. Add broth; bring to boiling. Reduce heat. Simmer, covered, 15 minutes or until farro is soft but still chewy in the center. Rinse with cold water; drain. Let cool.

STEP 2 Meanwhile, for dressing, remove 1 teaspoon zest and ¼ cup (50 mL) juice from lemon. In a screw-top jar combine the ½ cup oil (125 mL), lemon zest and juice, remaining shallot, oregano, salt, and pepper. Shake to combine. Toss half the dressing with the farro. Cover and chill remaining dressing until serving (let stand at room temperature about 30 minutes before serving if chilled).

STEP 3 In an extra-large serving dish combine farro mixture and the remaining ingredients. Cover; chill up to 24 hours. To serve, pour remaining dressing over salad; toss to coat.

EACH SERVING *442 cal, 26 g fat, 18 mg chol, 458 mg sodium, 41 g carb, 8 g fiber, 16 g pro*

155
BAKE BLUEBERRY TARTS

A rustic rye crust is the base for these blueberry-basil tarts. The dough is divided into four portions to make four small tarts—each of which serves three people.

PREP: 40 minutes CHILL: 1 hour BAKE: 30 minutes at 350°F (175°C) MAKES: 12 servings

1	cup (100 g) rye flour
1	cup (120 g) all-purpose flour
1	tablespoon sugar
¾	teaspoon salt
¾	cup (173 g) unsalted butter, cut up
½	cup (125 mL) ice water
⅓	cup (38 g) sliced almonds
¼	cup (24 g) whole wheat pastry flour
¼	cup (50 g) sugar
4	cups (600 g) fresh blueberries
5	tablespoons sugar
3	tablespoons finely snipped fresh basil
2	teaspoons lemon juice
1	egg, lightly beaten
¼	teaspoon ground cinnamon

STEP 1 For dough, in a bowl stir together the first four ingredients (through salt). Using a pastry blender, cut in butter until pieces are pea size. Sprinkle 1 tablespoon ice water over part of flour; toss with a fork. Push moistened pastry to side; repeat. Gather dough into a ball. Wrap in plastic wrap; chill 1 hour.

STEP 2 For filling, in a food processor combine almonds, pastry flour, and ¼ cup (50 g) sugar. Cover; process until almonds are finely ground. In a bowl combine blueberries, 3 tablespoons sugar, basil, and lemon juice.

STEP 3 Preheat oven to 350°F (175°C). Divide dough into four portions. For each tart, on a piece of floured parchment paper, roll one portion into a circle 8 inches (20 cm) in diameter. Slide onto a baking sheet. Sprinkle center with 3 tablespoons filling, leaving 1½-inch (4-cm) border uncovered. Top with 1 cup (250 mL) filling. Fold pastry edge over filling.

STEP 4 Brush pastry with egg. In a bowl combine remaining sugar and cinnamon. Sprinkle on top.

STEP 5 Bake 30 minutes or until pastry is golden and filling is bubbly.

EACH SERVING *265 cal, 14 g fat, 46 mg chol, 154 mg sodium, 34 g carb, 3 g fiber, 4 g pro*

CHAPTER 4

Fall

PUMPKINS

Pumpkins are a member of the squash family (*Cucurbita*) and there are many mini varieties to choose from—such as 'Jack-Be-Little' and white-skinned 'Baby Boo.' Planting pumpkins is a surefire way to get kids excited about gardening.

Pumpkins are synonymous with Halloween decor as well as the main pie ingredient at Thanksgiving, although most pumpkin fans have never actually eaten fresh pumpkin. And that's a shame—because fresh pumpkin is sweet, delicious, plentiful, and inexpensive in autumn. If you have a big patch of open flat land, you can grow pumpkins to use as autumn decor and in pumpkin recipes that range from soup to nuts (literally, because you can eat the seeds roasted to crisp, nutty perfection). Plant pumpkins in a spot that sees sun all day—at least 6 hours. The classic pumpkin hill is a slight hump planted with three to six seeds. Once the seeds germinate, pluck all but the most robust seedlings on each hill.

If you want the largest, highest-quality pumpkins, prune off extra fruits so each vine produces only a few. To raise pumpkins for eating, grow specific varieties for this purpose. Sweet, firm flesh can be baked, boiled, and sauteed. As with most deep-hued vegetables, pumpkins are rich in beta-carotene, an antioxidant.

156
PLANT, GROW & HARVEST

SITE Choose a large sunny spot so pumpkin plants can spread. Pumpkins do best in slightly acidic soil that drains easily.

BEDMATES Pumpkins can share space with corn, melons, and other squash. However, pumpkins are space hogs and need a lot of room on their own.

CARE Keep pumpkin vines free of weeds by shallow hoeing around plants.

HOW TO START Sow seeds directly in the ground when the soil/air temperatures reach at least 70°F (21°C). Start seeds ahead of the season and plant seedlings too.

HARVEST Begin harvest in late September or early October—before a hard frost. Pick pumpkins when they are a deep, solid color (depending on variety, this may be orange, white, or cream). Wear gloves (vines have prickles on the stems) and use pruning shears to cut each pumpkin from its vine. Leave 3 to 4 inches (8–10 cm) of stem attached and they will keep longer.

PESTS AND DISEASES Pumpkins are susceptible to fungal diseases such as powdery mildew. Treat with a fungicide. Insects attracted to pumpkins include cucumber beetles and squash bugs. If you use insecticides, apply in late afternoon or early evening after pumpkin blossoms have closed so bees are not adversely affected.

157 TAKE THESE TIPS TO THE GARDEN

158
KNOW YOUR VARIETIES

'LONG ISLAND CHEESE' A slightly flat, buff-orange pumpkin that resembles a wheel of cheese. The flesh is mild and sweet and excellent for pies. Fruits mature to 6 to 10 pounds (3–5 kg). Try 'Autumn Crown' for a mini version.

'SMALL SUGAR' The standard pumpkin-pie squash. It measures about 10 inches (25 cm) in diameter. The skin is orange-yellow and the flesh is sweet and fine-grained. It keeps well too.

'BABY PAM' This variety gets lots of votes for the best pie pumpkin. The 4-pound (2-kg) pumpkins have beautiful deep orange skins. The flesh is sweet and dry; each plant yields 4 to 5 pumpkins.

'BABY BEAR' A 1- to 2-pound (0.5–1 kg) deep orange pumpkin with a flat shape. Kids love harvesting this pumpkin because it's just the right size. It produces semihulless seeds that are ideal for roasting.

START Early in the season, start pumpkins indoors but don't plant pumpkin seeds (or seedlings) until after frost is past (A).

WATER Although pumpkins tolerate short periods of dry weather, if rainfall is scarce, water them. Create a slow-drip irrigation system by making a hole in an aluminum can and burying it next to the plant. Fill with water in drought situations (B).

BARRICADE Use mulch or straw to make a "pumpkin coaster," or barrier between the fruit and the ground to prevent rot. (C).

MOUND Form mounds of soil about 8 to 10 inches (20–25 cm) high and plant several seeds 1 inch (2.5 cm) deep in the top of the mound. Remove smaller seedlings when sprouts have 2 or 3 leaves. The ideal pumpkin hill should have 2 to 3 large plants per hill. Each hill should be 4 to 8 feet (1.2–2.5 m) apart.

159
STIR UP SOME PUMPKIN RISOTTO

Homemade pumpkin puree gives this creamy risotto its beautiful orange color and just a hint of sweetness. Flavored with Parmesan cheese and sage, it is the essence of fall.

PREP: 20 minutes   COOK: 45 minutes   MAKES: 4 servings

2	cups (475 mL) water
1¾	cups (425 mL) chicken broth
3	tablespoons unsalted butter
1	cup (150 g) finely chopped onion
1	clove garlic, minced
2	cups (394 g) arborio rice
1	cup (250 mL) dry white wine
1½	tablespoons snipped fresh sage
1	cup (227 g) Pumpkin Puree
½	cup (50 g) finely shredded Parmigiano-Reggiano cheese
	Shaved Parmigiano-Reggiano cheese
	Sage leaves (optional)

STEP 1 In a large saucepan bring water and broth to boiling; reduce heat to maintain simmer.

STEP 2 In a heavy 4-quart (4-L) pot melt butter over medium heat. Add onion and garlic; cook 3 minutes or until tender, stirring occasionally. Add rice; cook and stir 2 minutes. Add wine; cook and stir until liquid is absorbed. Stir in snipped sage and 1 cup (250 mL) of broth mixture; stir until almost all the liquid is absorbed. Continue cooking and adding broth, 1 cup (250 mL) at a time, until rice is tender but still firm to the bite and risotto is creamy.

STEP 3 Stir pumpkin puree and the ½ cup (50 g) cheese into risotto. Heat through, about 1 minute. Top with shaved cheese and, if desired, sage leaves.

STEP 4 Pumpkin Puree: Reheat oven to 375°F (190°C). Cut 2½ pounds (1 kg) pie pumpkins into 5×5-inch (13×13-cm) pieces. Remove and discard seeds and strings. Arrange pieces, skin sides up, in a foil-lined baking pan. Cover with foil. Bake 1 hour or until tender. Scoop pulp from rind. Place pulp in a food processor or blender. Cover and process or blend until smooth. Makes 1¾ cups (397 g).

EACH SERVING *385 cal, 11 g fat, 26 mg chol, 547 mg sodium, 61 g carb, 6 g fiber, 10 g pro*

160
BAKE A PUMPKIN-SWEET POTATO PIE

The crust for this fabulous pie is made from crumbled fig cookies! The toasty marshmallow topping is a nod to the nostalgic Thanksgiving sweet potato casserole.

PREP: 30 minutes   BAKE: 50 minutes at 350°F (175°C)   COOL: 1 hour   MAKES: 8 servings

8	fig cookies, approximately 6 ounces (170 g)
½	cup (60 g) all-purpose flour
4	tablespoons butter, melted
1	3-ounce (85-g) package cream cheese, softened
3	eggs
¾	cup (150 g) cooked and mashed sweet potatoes
¾	cup (170 g) fresh or canned pureed pumpkin
⅓	cup (60 g) packed brown sugar
⅓	cup (75 mL) whipping cream
¼	cup (50 g) granulated sugar
1	tablespoon molasses
2	teaspoons grated fresh ginger
1	teaspoon vanilla
1	teaspoon ground cinnamon
½	teaspoon salt
½	teaspoon freshly grated nutmeg or ¼ teaspoon ground nutmeg
⅛	teaspoon ground ancho or chipotle chile pepper
1½	cups (75 g) tiny marshmallows

STEP 1 Preheat oven to 350°F (175°C). For crust, in a bowl crumble together cookies and flour. Pour melted butter over the crumb mixture; stir. Press into the bottom and up the sides of a 9-inch (23-cm) pie pan. Bake 10 minutes or until set. Cool.

STEP 2 For filling, in a large bowl beat cream cheese with a mixer on medium for 30 seconds. Add the next 13 ingredients (through chile powder). Beat until well combined. Pour filling into pre-baked crust and bake 40 to 45 minutes or until a knife inserted near center comes out clean.

STEP 3 Remove pie from oven and top with a single layer of marshmallows. Preheat broiler. Broil pie 4 inches (10 cm) from heat for 1 to 2 minutes or just until marshmallows begin to brown.

STEP 4 Cool on a wire rack 1 hour before serving warm.

EACH SERVING *357 cal, 16 g fat, 110 mg chol, 348 mg sodium, 49 g carb, 2 g fiber, 5 g pro*

APPLES

Add apple trees to your landscape plan—a well-pruned tree offers flowers in the spring, provides apples during summer and fall, and lends an interesting shape to your yard during winter (once the leaves fall).

Apple trees (*Malus*) have three sizes: dwarf, semi-dwarf, and standard. Because apple tree varieties are generally grafted onto different rootstocks, you can usually pick the apple you want in one of these three sizes. The smallest apple trees are dwarfs that grow to about 10 feet (3 m) tall. Semi-dwarfs reach about 15 feet (4.6 m). And standard-size apple trees grow to 20 feet (6 m) or more.

For most small yards, dwarf and semi-dwarf apple trees are space-conscious choices. Once a dwarf apple tree begins producing fruit, it provides 3 to 6 bushels (57–114 kg) of fruit. A semi-dwarf tree can produce anywhere from 6 to 10 bushels (114–90 kg) of apples. With one bushel weighing 42 pounds (19 kg), at the minimum you'll get more than 100 pounds (45 kg) of apples from a dwarf tree.

For small spaces, grow trees in pots or train them to grow horizontally (a method called espalier). Columnar varieties are space-conscious and produce ample fruit. You may have to wait 3 to 5 years after planting for the first full harvest, but sweet, homegrown apples are worth the wait.

161
PLANT, GROW & HARVEST

SITE Apples require at least 6 hours of sun a day and well-drained soil.

BEDMATES Plant multiple apple trees for cross-pollination. Apples bear best when there are two varieties nearby. Some varieties have to be pollinated by another variety to bear fruit.

CARE Pruning apple trees yearly helps them keep their shape and encourages fruit production. In late winter prune apple trees to thin branches to 1 to 2 feet (30–61 cm) apart. Once trees set fruit, thin fruit by hand on full-size apple trees, one apple per spur. Fertilize apple trees with a general-purpose timed-release plant food each spring.

HOW TO START Buy bare-root or container-grown apple trees.

HARVEST Apples ripen in 70 to 180 days from bloom, depending on variety. Pick apples from the tree when they separate easily from the branch and have firm flesh. Soft apples can be used for cooking. Store them in a cool spot after harvest.

PESTS AND DISEASES Early-season apples are the most susceptible to apple maggot. Spray infestations with insecticidal soap. Use dormant oil spray in late winter (before buds swell) to control codling moths, plum curculios, scale, leaf rollers, mites, and aphids.

162 TAKE THESE TIPS TO THE GARDEN

PLANT In late spring, plant apple trees after the soil is thawed. Dig a hole 2 feet (61 cm) wider than the spread of the tree roots; plant at the same depth as it was in the nursery pot. Keep the graft union 2 inches (5 cm) above the soil line (A).

TRAIN Young trees can be trained to a modified central leader. Thin branches to 1 to 2 inches (3–5 cm) apart. To train apples against a wall or building—espalier—start with a young tree (B).

GROW Apple trees can be grown in containers. Try dwarf and columnar varieties (C).

PRUNE Each year during the dormant season, work at creating wide crotch angles, which are less prone to breaking.

THINNING Removing apples growing really close together results in larger mature fruit.

164
KNOW YOUR EARLY FALL APPLE VARIETIES

'ANNA' This variety produces green apples with red blush. This early-season apple is suited for warmer climates. Pair it with early-flowering varieties to ensure pollination.

'ROYAL GALA' Introduced to North America from New Zealand, this crisp, juicy apple has red striping on its yellow-tinged skin. An early producer, it ripens in August. A delicious apple for eating out of hand, it is also good for pies, crisps, and applesauce.

'GINGER GOLD' An early-ripening apple. Sweet, firm, and delicious, 'Ginger Gold' doesn't keep long, so enjoy while you have them.

'LODI' A green-skinned apple and one of the earliest to produce. It's also among the best of the cooking apples.

163
KNOW YOUR MID-FALL APPLE VARIETIES

'JONATHAN' A small to medium crisp, dark red apple with a tart flavor. A good all-purpose apple.

'GOLDEN DELICIOUS' This variety produces firm, crisp, round apples. The flesh is sweet and juicy—great for all occasions.

'MCINTOSH' This variety bears medium to large bright red apples with sweet, juicy white flesh and can be prepared many ways.

'LADY' An heirloom variety with excellent storage ability. The small to medium fruit has green skin with red blush and ripens late in the season.

'HONEYCRISP' This variety produces medium fruit and has a crisp, juicy texture and a sweet flavor with a touch of tartness.

'GRANNY SMITH' Glossy bright green fruit that is medium to large in size. It has a very tart flavor.

165
MAKE MINI APPLE AND PEAR TARTS

Puff pastry makes quick work of these tiny tarts. A splash of bourbon and a sprinkle of sea salt enhances the flavor of the roasted fall fruit.

PREP: 20 minutes   ROAST: 32 minutes at 425°F (220°C)   MAKES: 9 servings

- ½   cup (99 g) packed brown sugar
- ¼   cup (58 g) butter, melted
- ½   teaspoon ground cinnamon
- 2   cups (200 g) sliced apples and/or pears
- 1   tablespoon bourbon (optional)
- ½   17.3-ounce (490-g) package (1 sheet) frozen puff pastry sheets, thawed
- ¼   cup (29 g) chopped walnuts or pecans, toasted*
-      Sea salt flakes (optional)

STEP 1 Preheat oven to 425°F (220°C). In a small bowl combine brown sugar, melted butter, and cinnamon. Spread in a 13×9-inch (33×23-cm) baking pan. Top with apples. Roast 15 minutes. Remove fruit. If desired, stir bourbon into sugar mixture in pan.

STEP 2 Line a baking sheet with parchment paper. On a lightly floured surface, unfold puff pastry and cut into nine 3-inch squares (8-cm). Using a paring knife, make a shallow cut around each square ½ inch (1 cm) from the edges. Generously prick centers with a fork. Place 1 inch (3 cm) apart on prepared baking sheet. Roast 10 minutes. Press down centers with back of a spoon.

STEP 3 Spoon apples into centers of tarts. Drizzle fruit in each tart with 2 teaspoons of the sugar mixture. Sprinkle with walnuts. Roast 7 to 10 minutes more or until the pastry is lightly browned. Drizzle tarts with remaining sugar mixture and, if desired, sprinkle with a little salt.

*TIP To toast walnuts, preheat oven to 350°F (175°). Spread walnuts in a shallow baking pan. Bake 5 to 10 minutes or until nuts are lightly browned, shaking pan once or twice.

EACH SERVING *284 cal, 18 g fat, 14 mg chol, 112 mg sodium, 30 g carb, 2 g fiber, 2 g pro*

166
GO DUTCH WITH AN APPLE PANCAKE

Also known as a Dutch baby, this puffed oven pancake filled with glazed apples makes an impressive breakfast. Kids will like watching the pancake inflate as it bakes.

PREP: 5 minutes   BAKE: 20 minutes at 400°F (200°C)   COOK: 5 minutes   MAKES: 6 servings

8	tablespoons butter
4	eggs
1	cup (120 g) all-purpose flour
1	cup (250 mL) milk
¼	teaspoon ground nutmeg or ground cinnamon
	Dash salt
3	medium apples, peeled, cored, and thinly sliced
½	cup (99 g) packed brown sugar
¼	teaspoon ground nutmeg or ground cinnamon (optional)
	Powdered sugar or whipped cream (optional)

STEP 1 Preheat oven to 400°F (200°C). For batter, place 6 tablespoons of the butter in a 10-inch (25-cm) ovenproof skillet (preferably cast iron). Place in oven until butter is melted. In a medium bowl lightly beat eggs until combined. Add flour, milk, ¼ teaspoon nutmeg, and the salt; beat until smooth. Immediately pour batter into the hot skillet. Bake 20 to 25 minutes or until puffed and well browned.

STEP 2 Meanwhile, for filling, in a saucepan melt the remaining 2 tablespoons butter. Add apples; cook over medium heat until apples are almost tender, stirring frequently. Add brown sugar and, if desired, ¼ teaspoon nutmeg. Cook and stir until apples are glazed. Remove from heat.

STEP 3 To serve, transfer pancake to a large serving platter. Spoon filling into the center of the pancake. If desired, sprinkle with sifted powdered sugar or top with whipped cream. Serve immediately.

EACH SERVING *278 cal, 17 fat, 133 mg chol, 235 mg sodium, 24 g carb, 1 g fiber, 5 g pro*

POTATOES

So easy to grow and so delicious, you'll want to have hills of potatoes in your garden. *Solanum tuberosum* is an annual vegetable crop planted in early spring and harvested in late summer through autumn. It takes 2 to 4 months for the crop to mature, but you harvest "new" potatoes in as little as 6 weeks. These subterranean tubers are grown from seed potatoes, which are pieces of mature potatoes. With more than 4,000 types of potatoes to choose from, you won't have any trouble finding one or several to grow.

Potatoes, originally from Peru, are part of nearly every culture's cuisine and play a large role in the world's favorite dishes. The earthy taste of freshly dug potatoes is sublime, and plucked from your backyard garden, these tender gems can be prepared boiled, roasted, fried, and mashed.

Potato varieties offer a rainbow of colors (skin and flesh can be different hues). Potatoes can have skins that are red, white, yellow, or purple. Flesh color can be blue, yellow, or snow white. Potatoes also have a wide variety of sizes, from small fingerlings to giant spuds that weigh several pounds each. Flesh consistency is different too, and that influences how to cook them. For example, floury potatoes are used for baking and have more starch than waxy potatoes, which are better for boiling.

167
PLANT, GROW & HARVEST

SITE Potatoes need a sunny location with well-drained soil.

BEDMATES Rotate growing beds. Don't plant potatoes where tomatoes or eggplant were grown; they are in the same family and may attract similar pests.

CARE Keep the soil in the potato bed consistently moist but not wet. Potatoes require fertilizer higher in phosphorus and potassium than nitrogen. Begin mounding (hilling) soil around the bottom of stems when plants reach 6 inches (15 cm) tall. Cover potatoes poking out of the soil or they will turn green and develop a toxin.

HOW TO START Plant potatoes from seed potatoes or pieces of sprouting tubers.

HARVEST Early potato varieties can be dug when the tubers are 1 to 2 inches (2.5–5 cm) in diameter. To grow larger potatoes, wait until the plant tops start to die back, then harvest. Store potatoes in a dark, humid location for 2 weeks. For long-term storage, 40°F to 50°F (4–10°C).

PESTS AND DISEASES Scab can be prevented by keeping soil pH acidic. Use a fungicide to prevent anthracnose. Pick off and destroy beetles, worms, and caterpillars. Use Bt or neem if insect infestations get out of hand. Use insecticidal soap to control leafhoppers, and floating row covers to protect young plants.

168 TAKE THESE TIPS TO THE GARDEN

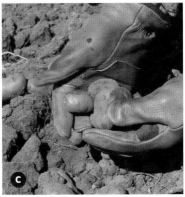

PLANT Cut up whole potatoes into pieces that have "eyes." Allow pieces to dry overnight. Place the cut potatoes in a 4- to 6-inch (10–15-cm) trench with the eyes up. Space rows 12 to 15 inches (30–38 cm) apart (A).

HILL Mound the soil around the base of the stems as the potato plants get larger. This gives more underground space for the potatoes to grow (B).

HARVEST Unearth new potatoes by digging down beside the stem and removing individual tubers (C). Harvest new (or young and small) potatoes 6 to 8 weeks after planting.

DIG You can dig out mature potatoes can with a fork, taking care not to spear them as you unearth them (D).

169 KNOW YOUR VARIETIES

'ALL BLUE' Blue outside and in, this medium-size potato really gives a meal color. Try it steamed, sauteed, or sliced and diced in a gratin dish.

'CRANBERRY RED' Also known as 'All Red,' this large potato features smooth, moist texture and is excellent steamed or sauteed.

'ELBA' This large white-skin, white-flesh variety is tops for baking or boiling. It's also a treat in salads because it holds its shape well when cooked.

'ISLAND SUNSHINE' With golden-white skin and golden flesh, this medium-size round potato tastes good baked or fried.

'ONAWAY' A round white potato, this variety is a reliable grower and ripens early. Its moist texture and shape hold up when boiled.

'REDDALE' Blushing red on the outside and white inside, this large potato has moist flesh that's well suited for boiling.

'ROSE GOLD' This potato boasts rosy red skin and golden flesh. It's high in starch, so it's ideal to bake, steam, or use in cream soups.

'RUSSIAN BANANA' This golden-skin fingerling potato with crescent-shape tapered ends is especially tasty baked, boiled, and in salads.

'YUKON GOLD' This golden-flesh potato is an especially good keeper and all-around winner. It's ideal for baking, frying, and boiling.

There are hundreds of potato varieties in all colors of the rainbow. If an award were given to the most versatile vegetable, the potato would have it locked.

170
HEAT UP WITH A WARM POTATO SALAD

This delicious departure from classic potato salad features creamy Dutch yellow potatoes, caramelized onions, and a chile vinaigrette made with roasted Anaheim peppers.

PREP: 30 minutes   ROAST: 25 minutes at 425°F (220°C)   MAKES: 12 servings

- 3 pounds (1.5 kg) Dutch yellow potatoes, halved
- 5 tablespoons olive oil
  Kosher salt and black pepper
- 1 large sweet onion, thinly sliced
- 1 tablespoon butter
- ½ cup (125 mL) seasoned rice vinegar
- 2 tablespoons sugar
- 1½ pounds (700 g) Anaheim chiles, roasted*, cooled, coarsely chopped
- 1 clove garlic, peeled
- ⅓ cup (75 mL) canola oil
  Fresh cilantro

STEP 1 Preheat oven to 425°F (220°C). For potato salad, in a shallow roasting pan toss together potatoes and 3 tablespoons of the olive oil. Season with salt and pepper. Roast potatoes, uncovered, 25 to 30 minutes or until easily pierced with a fork. Let cool.

STEP 2 Meanwhile, to caramelize onions, in a large skillet heat the remaining olive oil and the butter. Add onion slices; cook 15 minutes or until golden, stirring frequently.

STEP 3 For vinaigrette, in a blender combine vinegar, sugar, ½ cup (125 mL) of the roasted chiles, and garlic. Cover; blend until combined. With blender running, add canola oil until thickened. Season with salt and black pepper.

STEP 4 In a bowl toss roasted potatoes, caramelized onions, and remaining chopped chiles. Add 1 cup (250 mL) of the vinaigrette; toss to combine. Sprinkle salad with cilantro. Pass remaining vinaigrette.

*TIP To roast peppers, preheat oven to 425°F (220°C). Arrange peppers on a baking sheet. Roast 20 minutes or until skins are blistered and browned.

EACH SERVING *284 cal, 15 g fat, 3 mg chol, 202 mg sodium, 35 g carb, 5 g fiber, 4 g pro*

171
ROAST YOUR ROOTS

The presence of chickpeas in this medley of roasted root vegetables makes it suitable as either a hearty side dish or a vegetarian entree.

PREP: 30 minutes   ROAST: 45 minutes at 425°F (220°C)   MAKES: 8 servings

1	pound (450 g) carrots, peeled and cut in 2-inch (5-cm) pieces
1	pound (450 g) sweet potatoes, peeled and cut in chunks
1	large red onion, peeled, halved, and cut in 1-inch (2.5-cm) wedges
1	pound (450 g) red or russet potatoes, cut in cubes
6	cloves garlic, minced
1	16-ounce (450-g) can chickpeas (garbanzo beans), rinsed and drained
2	to 3 tablespoons olive oil
1	teaspoon dried rosemary, crushed
1	teaspoon packed brown sugar or granulated sugar
½	teaspoon kosher salt
½	teaspoon freshly ground black pepper

STEP 1 Position an oven rack in the center of oven. Preheat oven to 425°F (220°C). Place all vegetables, garlic, and chickpeas in a large shallow roasting pan. In a small bowl combine the oil, rosemary, brown sugar, salt, and pepper. Drizzle over vegetables; toss well to coat.

STEP 2 Roast, uncovered, 45 minutes or until vegetables are lightly browned and tender, stirring twice.

EACH SERVING *223 cal, 4 g fat, 0 mg chol, 301 mg sodium, 42 g carb, 7 g fiber, 6 g pro*

PEARS

Pears are one of the world's oldest cultivated fruits. Prized for their sweet taste, versatility, and long storage life, pears date back more than 7,000 years. Pear trees can be trained into formal or informal appearance—and they are one of the easiest fruit trees to grow. For small landscapes or a kitchen garden, choose the smallest pear, a dwarf. If you have space for one tree, select a self-pollinating (or self-fruitful) type. Otherwise pears need a pollinator, and more than one is required. Make sure they are compatible with each other.

Pear trees bloom in spring and produce small white buds that unfurl into single-petal white flowers. If there is a late frost while the tree is in flower, it often means there will be no fruit for the year. The fruit of the pear tree is produced on spurs, which appear on shoots more than 1 year old.

For fresh fruit or to can the bounty, a pear will not disappoint. These big producers bear bushels of succulent fruit. Harvest pears when they are mature but still hard, and let them ripen at room temperature for the best quality. Firm varieties, such as 'Bosc' or 'Anjou,' are best choices for poaching, baking, and grilling because their dense flesh holds shape. Soft pears, such as 'Yellow Bartlett,' 'Red Bartlett,' and 'Comice,' are better candidates for eating fresh.

172
PLANT, GROW & HARVEST

SITE Choose a sunny, well-drained location. Pears are deep rooted and can grow in any soil but do best in rich, heavy loam.

BEDMATES If you plant one pear, choose a self-pollinating type. Otherwise, pears need a cross pollinator—two or more varieties.

CARE Feed newly planted pear trees after the soil around the roots is thoroughly settled (2 to 3 weeks after planting).

HOW TO START Plant bare-root or container-grown trees.

HARVEST Pear trees bear fruit based on size. Standard trees produce fruit in 5 to 6 years; dwarf trees bear fruit faster—in just 3 to 4 years. Pick pears in August through September, 1 to 2 weeks before completely ripe. Pears should ripen at room temperature. To store fresh pears, keep them in a cool, dark place.

PESTS AND DISEASES Pear trees are susceptible to fire blight. Prune off affected branches and destroy. Fire blight is a bacterial disease with no cure. Another disease, pear psylla, can be controlled by spraying with dormant oil spray in late winter or early spring. To control pear scab and pests, rake up and remove windfall fruits and leaves. Protect tree trunks from bark-eating rabbits or mice by wrapping hardware cloth or plastic guards around the lower portion of trunks.

173 TAKE THESE TIPS TO THE GARDEN

(A)

PLANT For a bare-root or container-grown pear tree, dig a hole large enough to allow the roots to spread out completely. Backfill the planting hole with topsoil.

DWARF PEAR TREES These trees have graft unions (where the variety was grafted onto rootstock); make sure when planting that these are 2 to 3 inches (5–8 cm) above the soil surface (A).

PRUNE Pears trees don't need to be pruned as much as other fruit trees. However, you should prune standard trees to a central leader. In late winter or early spring, head back side branches so they don't compete with the central leader.

GROW Dwarf varieties make excellent hedges, or prune them into espalier forms.

THIN After normal fruit drop, thin the remaining fruits for best size.

174
KNOW YOUR VARIETIES

'BARTLETT' This popular pear bears large yellow fruit with smooth, juicy white flesh.

'BOSC' This variety has a unique sweet-spice flavor and brown skin. These firm fruits have a long neck and a full rounded base.

'HOSUI ASIAN' A round pear with a snappy tang for taste. The blight-resistant tree is self-pollinating.

'KIEFFER' An oval Oriental pear with yellow-green skin splashed in red when ripe. The white flesh is crisp and juicy with coarse texture.

'SECKEL' This variety produces small fruit early in the season with intense sweet flavor. They store well and the trees are resistant to fire blight.

'SHINKO ASIAN' The fruit is sweet and juicy, and the tree is an excellent producer that bears medium to large fruit with golden-brown skin and creamy flesh.

There are more than 3000 varieties of pear trees grown worldwide — evidence that pears are one of the world's favorite fruits.

175
POACH PEARS FOR DESSERT

These pears, poached in white wine flavored with orange peel, cinnamon, and star anise, then topped with vanilla crème fraîche—make a light and elegant dessert after a hearty fall meal.

PREP: 10 minutes COOK: 15 minutes MAKES: 4 servings

3	cups (700 mL) dry white wine
1	cup (250 mL) sugar
1	cup (250 mL) water
4	strips orange peel
3	inches (8 cm) stick cinnamon
2	whole star anise
4	firm ripe pears, peeled and cored, leaving stem intact
¼	cup (50 mL) crème fraîche
¼	cup (50 mL) whipping cream
1	teaspoon vanilla bean paste or vanilla extract

STEP 1 In a large heavy saucepan combine wine, sugar, water, orange peel, cinnamon, and star anise. Bring to boiling. Add pears to saucepan. Return to boiling; reduce heat. Simmer, covered, 15 to 20 minutes or until pears are tender.

STEP 2 For vanilla crème fraîche, in a small bowl whisk together crème fraîche, whipping cream, and vanilla bean paste until light.

STEP 3 To serve, remove pears from syrup; reserve syrup. Cut pears lengthwise in half. Divide the pear halves among 4 shallow dessert dishes. Spoon about ¼ cup (50 mL) syrup over each. Top with vanilla crème fraîche. Serve immediately.

EACH SERVING *373 cal, 11 g fat, 41 mg chol, 18 mg sodium, 53 g carb, 5 g fiber, 1 g pro*

176
PAIR PEARS WITH ENDIVE

The leaves of endive are natural scoops for a filling of pear, walnuts, and goat cheese for this easy appetizer.

START TO FINISH: 25 minutes   **MAKES:** 6 servings

1   tablespoon olive oil

2   teaspoons lemon juice
    Salt and black pepper

1   firm medium pear, such as
    Bartlett, cored and thinly sliced
    lengthwise

¼   cup (29 g) coarsely chopped
    walnuts (toasted if desired)

¼   cup (6 g) loosely packed fresh
    parsley leaves

4   ounces (115 g) goat cheese,
    crumbled

12 endive leaves (1 large head)
    Honey (optional)

STEP 1 In a medium bowl whisk
together oil and lemon juice.
Season with salt and pepper. Add
pear, walnuts, parsley, and goat
cheese. Toss to coat.

STEP 2 Spoon pear mixture into
endive leaves. Arrange stuffed
leaves on a serving platter. If
desired, drizzle with honey.

EACH SERVING *140 cal, 11 g fat,*
15 mg chol, 197 mg sodium, 6 g carb,
1 g fiber, 5 g pro

GARLIC

Fragrant and pungent, hot and strong, garlic adds depth of flavor to a variety of foods. So popular, this edible bulb often gets top billing in recipes—garlic mashed potatoes, garlic bread, garlic chicken. This flavorful vegetable is used like an herb—as a seasoning. Roasted, garlic takes on a mild, nutty flavor and spreadable consistency. Use raw garlic in salad dressings and sauces to add unmistakable zip.

Hardneck garlic is the hardiest form. Varieties in this group form cloves around a woody stem that sends up a curly flower stalk. Softneck garlic forms cloves around a soft neck or stem, which braids easily. The typical lifespan of garlic (*Allium sativum*) is very different from most vegetables. First bulbs are planted in fall and harvested the following year. After planting the garlic bulbs, which look very much like tulip or daffodil bulbs, garlic sets roots and sits out the winter underground. In spring, garlic sends up a shoot and may even start to bloom—tiny would-be flowers are called scapes. Remove them before the buds open to make the plant put more energy into the clove (for bigger and better harvests). Scapes have mild garlic flavor and are edible—saute them in a little butter or olive oil for an early taste of what's to come.

177
PLANT, GROW & HARVEST

SITE Garlic prefers a spot in full sun and moist, well-drained soil.

BEDMATES Rotate crops every year to prevent disease.

CARE Amend soil each year with compost. Because garlic has a shallow root system, water well in spring when the cloves are developing; stop watering in July to allow the foliage to die back before harvest; and keep weeds under control.

HOW TO START Garlic is grown from the cloves. The larger the clove, the larger the bulb it produces. The best time to plant garlic is in the fall after your area's first killing frost. The following spring garlic sends up shoots. Plant individual garlic cloves 1 inch (2.5 cm) deep and 6 inches (15 cm) apart with the points up.

HARVEST Many gardeners wait to harvest until plant growth has turned brown—usually August or September. Carefully dig up the bulbs and lift them out of the ground with a garden fork. Cut leaves back to 1 inch (2.5 cm) tall and brush off the soil to clean them. Leave garlic to dry in a warm spot for 4 weeks to cure.

PESTS AND DISEASES Because most of the major diseases affecting garlic are found in the soil, yearly crop rotation of garlic beds helps produce healthy garlic. To avoid fungus, space plants to ensure good air circulation.

178 TAKE THESE TIPS TO THE GARDEN

REMOVE Garlic scapes should be cut off to put more of the plant's power into making a bigger bulb (A).

SEPARATE Just before planting, separate the cloves from the bulb; don't separate them beforehand (B).

SPREAD After planting garlic, spread a couple inches of mulch over the soil to help prevent injury to the plants from sudden cold spells in fall or spring (C). Mulch will also deter weeds in spring and help the soil conserve moisture.

STORE Garlic should be stored in a cool spot (lower than 40°F/4°C) until you can use it (D). Properly cured garlic will usually hold for about 6 months.

179 KNOW YOUR VARIETIES

'NEW YORK WHITE' Also called 'Polish White,' 'New York White' is a hardy, disease-resistant variety for cool climates.

'RUSSIAN RED' A hardneck type with purple stripes on its cloves. It is exceptionally winter hardy.

'SILVER WHITE' A softneck type for warm climates. It produces easy-to-peel white bulbs.

'SPANISH ROJA' A hardneck type with medium-hot flavor. The brown-skin cloves are excellent for roasting.

Elephant garlic is very large and has about four cloves to a bulb. It is closely related to the leek and has a milder flavor than regular garlic.

180
TOP SOUP WITH GARLIC TOAST

This white bean-escarole soup is flavored with leeks, fennel, and onion. Roasting the garlic turns it creamy and sweet.

PREP: 20 minutes   ROAST: 30 minutes at 400°F (200°C)   COOK: 30 minutes   MAKES: 6 servings

2	bulbs garlic
1	teaspoon olive oil
2	medium leeks, chopped
1	cup (100 g) chopped fennel
⅓	cup (50 g) chopped onion
3	tablespoons olive oil
3	cups (700 mL) vegetable broth
2	15-ounce (425-g) cans cannellini beans (white kidney beans), rinsed and drained
1	cup (250 mL) half-and-half
3	tablespoons lemon juice
	Salt and black pepper
6	½-inch (1 cm) slices baguette-style French bread
6	slices Swiss cheese
½	head escarole, torn

STEP 1 Preheat oven to 400°F (200°C). Peel off papery layer of bulbs. Cut off top third of bulbs, exposing tops of cloves. Place bulbs in the middle of a piece of foil; drizzle bulbs with 1 teaspoon oil; fold foil to form a packet. Roast 30 to 35 minutes or until soft. Let cool 30 minutes. Squeeze cloves from bulbs into a bowl; mash with a fork.

STEP 2 In a saucepan cook leeks, fennel, and onion in 1 tablespoon oil over medium heat for 15 to 20 minutes or until caramelized. Add half of the roasted garlic, the broth, and 1½ cans of the beans. Bring to boiling; reduce heat. Simmer, covered, 15 minutes. Place mixture in a food processor. Process until smooth; return to

saucepan. Add remaining beans, half-and-half, and 2 tablespoons lemon juice. Cook over low heat until heated through. Season with salt and pepper.

STEP 4 Meanwhile, preheat broiler. Place baguette slices on a baking sheet. Broil 1 to 2 minutes or until lightly toasted, turning once. Spread toast with remaining

roasted garlic. Top with a cheese slice. Broil until cheese melts.

STEP 5 In a bowl whisk together remaining oil and lemon juice. Season with salt and pepper. Add escarole; toss to coat. Top servings with escarole and toasts.

EACH SERVING *387 cal, 17 g fat, 28 mg chol, 990 mg sodium, 42 g carb, 9 g fiber, 16 g pro*

181
BUILD A BETTER BURGER WITH GARLIC

No ordinary patty, this burger is infused with a roasted garlic paste stirred together with Parmesan cheese, onion, dried tomatoes, and basil before being grilled and topped with melty fresh mozzarella.

PREP: 20 minutes   ROAST: 30 minutes at 400°F (200°C)   COOL: 30 minutes   GRILL: 20 minutes   STAND: 2 minutes   MAKES: 6 servings

2	bulbs garlic
1	tablespoon olive oil
¾	cup (75 g) freshly grated Parmesan cheese
⅓	cup (50 g) finely chopped onion
⅓	cup (37 g) snipped, drained oil-packed dried tomatoes
½	cup (7 g) snipped fresh basil
½	teaspoon black pepper
¼	teaspoon salt
1½	pounds (700 g) 85 percent lean ground beef
8	ounces (225 g) bulk Italian sausage
6	ounces (170 g) fresh mozzarella
6	ciabatta rolls, split
	Fresh baby spinach leaves
½	cup (113 g) mayonnaise

STEP 1 Preheat oven to 400°F (200°C). Peel off papery layer of garlic bulbs. Cut off top third of bulbs, exposing tops of cloves. Place bulbs in the center of a piece of foil; drizzle with oil; fold foil to form a packet. Roast 30 to 35 minutes or until soft. Let cool 30 minutes. Squeeze cloves from bulbs into a bowl; mash with a fork.

STEP 2 In a bowl combine the garlic and the next seven ingredients. Add ground beef and sausage. Mix lightly. Shape into twelve ½-inch (12-mm) patties, 4 inches (10 cm) wide. Cut the mozzarella into six ¼-inch (6-mm) slices, then top six patties with a mozzarella slice. Top each with one remaining patty. Pinch edges of patties together.

STEP 3 Arrange grill for indirect grilling with medium heat around a drip pan. Grill patties over pan, covered, 20 minutes or until done (160°F/71°C), turning once.

STEP 4 Brush cut side of rolls with oil and toast, cut sides down, the last 2 minutes of grilling.

STEP 5 Serve patties on rolls with spinach leaves and mayo.

EACH SERVING *876 cal, 67 g fat, 145 mg chol, 1,101 mg sodium, 27 g carb, 2 g fiber, 39 g pro*

ONIONS

Growing onions in the garden is so easy—and such a treat. Large onions, sometimes called storage onions, need time—up to 110 days—to grow. When you harvest the juicy bulbs in mid to late summer, they've gained heft and flavor from growing subterraneanly. Enjoy them well into winter.

With so many varieties of onions to choose from—yellow, white, and red—you may want to plant several types to see which you like best. Onions offer a wide range of flavors. Yellow onions have a hot, complex flavor due to high sulfur levels and they saute to a rich brown and sweeten when cooked. Mild and sweet 'Vidalia,' 'Walla Walla,' and 'Maui' onions have higher water content and can be eaten raw by the slice or develop extra flavor when grilled. Red onions are sweet enough to eat raw; they offer splashes of bright color to potato or other vegetable salads. White onions have a clean, tangy taste; chop them and toss into salads and over tacos.

Onions are part of the large and diverse *Allium* genus of pungent edibles, such as chives, shallots, scallions, and garlic, as well as inedible garden flowers such as the purple-flower *Allium giganteum*. The edible onion is *Allium cepa*. Sometimes called small onions, shallots are small, more garlicky, and best cooked in sauces or sautes. Many people find them too hot to dice and eat raw.

182
PLANT, GROW & HARVEST

SITE Onions prefer to grow in a sunny spot in well-drained soil.

BEDMATES Plant onions with carrots, leeks, beets, kohlrabi, strawberries, Brassicas, dill, lettuce, and tomatoes.

CARE Hand weeding is best around young onions because they have shallow root systems. Keep well watered, but not too wet.

HOW TO START Grow onions from sets, transplants, or seeds. Onion seedlings can be purchased in bundles and planted directly in the garden. Or sow onion seeds indoors in flats in early spring; when seedlings are 4 inches (10 cm) tall, transplant into beds.

HARVEST When foliage begins to die back, stop watering. About a week later, pull bulbs out of the ground and let them cure for a few days in a warm, airy spot on a layer of newspapers. When the outer skin becomes crispy dry, the onions have cured. Hang onion bunches or place them in mesh bags. Store in a cool, dry place. Onions last for several months. Harvest shallots after side bulbs have formed and tops have begun to dry. Separate side bulbs; dry and store as you would onions.

PESTS AND DISEASES Onions can get a number of diseases, most of which are caused by prolonged wet conditions. Some fungus species affect onions, and neck rot affects stored onions.

183 TAKE THESE TIPS TO THE GARDEN

GROW Onions can be grown in containers. Just poke seedlings around other veggies (A).

PLANT To ensure the largest and tastiest harvests, plant onions early in the season.

HARVEST Short-rooted shallots are easy to harvest—give them a tug and they pop right out of the ground.

CURE Onions need to cure for a few days after digging them up. Lay out onions in a warm, airy spot. When the outer skin becomes papery and crispy dry, the onions have cured (B).

GROW There are specific onion varieties suited specifically to your climate. Grow long-day types in the cool climates and short-day types in the warm climates. Or plant intermediate-day types anywhere.

HARVEST Onions are mature and ready to harvest in mid to late summer. Watch for the green plant top to start to wither and turn brown—the foliage may collapse onto the ground (C). Don't allow mature onions to sit in wet soil—they rot rapidly.

184
KNOW YOUR ONION VARIETIES

'CANDY HYBRID' A mild-flavor yellow intermediate-day onion. It stores well and is ready in 85 days.

'COPRA HYBRID' A widely adapted long-day yellow storage onion that matures in 105 days. Sweeter than most storage onions.

'GIANT RED HAMBURGER' A dark red bulb, good for slicing. Its interior flesh is white and sweet. It is best adapted to warm climates and ready to pick in 95 days.

'REDWING HYBRID' This variety has pungent, red-flesh bulbs that store well. It's ready to harvest 110 days after planting.

'SUPERSTAR HYBRID' This variety has white bulbs that weigh up to 1 pound (450 g). It is day neutral, so can be planted anywhere, and is ready in 100 days.

185
KNOW YOUR SHALLOT VARIETIES

'AMBITION' SHALLOT This variety produces divided bulbs with reddish-copper skin and white flesh that are ready to pick 90 days after planting.

'GOLDEN GOURMET' A mild-tasting, high-yielding shallot that keeps well and is ready to harvest 77 days after planting.

186
ROAST ONIONS AND FENNEL WITH PROSCIUTTO

Red onions turn sweet and tender when roasted in this side dish that features anise-flavored fennel and crispy prosciutto. Try it with roast pork or beef.

PREP: 20 minutes   **ROAST:** 35 minutes at 400°F (200°C)   **MAKES:** 6 servings

3   medium fennel bulbs, trimmed and cut into 1-inch (2.5-cm) wedges

2   medium red onions, cut into 1-inch (2.5-cm) wedges

2   tablespoons olive oil

¼   teaspoon salt

¼   teaspoon black pepper

2   ounces (57 g) prosciutto, cut into shreds

2   tablespoons finely shredded Asiago cheese

1   teaspoon snipped fresh thyme
      Snipped fennel fronds

STEP 1 Preheat oven to 400°F (200°C). In a shallow baking pan combine fennel and onion wedges. Drizzle with oil and sprinkle with salt and pepper; toss to coat.

STEP 2 Roast 35 to 40 minutes or until tender and light brown, stirring occasionally. Sprinkle with remaining ingredients.

EACH SERVING *132 cal, 8 g fat, 3 mg chol, 353 mg sodium, 12 g carb, 4 g fiber, 5 g pro*

187
ROCK THE CROCK WITH ROASTED ONION SOUP

One of the world's best-loved soups features the humble onion. This version of the French favorite calls for roasting rather than sautéeing the onions to caramelize and sweeten them.

PREP: 25 minutes   ROAST: 45 minutes at 375°F (190°C)   COOK: 20 minutes   MAKES: 4 servings

2	large sweet onions, sliced
1	tablespoon olive oil
1	tablespoon butter, melted
2	cloves garlic, minced
¼	teaspoon salt
¼	teaspoon black pepper
4	cups (1 L) reduced-sodium beef broth
1	tablespoon dry sherry (optional)
1	teaspoon Worcestershire sauce
8	slices French bread, toasted
8	ounces (225 g) shredded Gruyère cheese
	Snipped fresh thyme (optional)

STEP 1 Preheat oven to 375°F (190°C). Place onions in a 13×9-inch (33×23-cm) baking pan. Drizzle with oil and melted butter and sprinkle with garlic, salt, and pepper; toss to coat. Roast 45 to 50 minutes or until very tender and light brown, stirring occasionally.

STEP 2 Carefully pour 1 cup (250 mL) of the broth into pan, stirring to scrape up any crusty brown bits. Transfer onion mixture to a large saucepan. Add remaining 3 cups (700 mL) broth, sherry (if desired), and Worcestershire sauce. Bring to boiling; reduce heat. Simmer, covered, 20 minutes.

STEP 3 Preheat broiler. Line a baking sheet with foil. Place bread slices on prepared baking sheet; sprinkle with cheese. Broil 4 inches (10 cm) from heat 3 to 4 minutes or until cheese is lightly browned. Serve soup topped with bread slices and, if desired, snipped fresh thyme.

EACH SERVING *514 cal, 26 g fat, 70 mg chol, 1,376 mg sodium, 43 g carb, 3 g fiber, 27 g pro*

BRUSSELS SPROUTS

If you're a fan of Brussels sprouts but have yet to raise them or see them growing, you are in for a surprise. They don't look or grow like any other vegetable. Brussels sprout plants have thick, trunklike stalks that grow 2 to 3 feet (61–91 cm) tall. They look like little trees.

Brussels sprouts (*Brassica oleracea* Gemmifera Group) are members of the cabbage family. The round cabbagelike sprouts grow up the stalk, studding the entire length. Each stalk can produce 50 to 100 sprouts. In short, Brussels sprouts are a showstopper in the garden. And if you have kids, you should add a couple Brussels sprouts plants to your vegetable garden if only for the surprise factor. Kids love to harvest these little cabbages, which are easy to pluck off the massive stem. Another reason to grow Brussels sprouts is that they are one of the last crops to harvest from the garden. You can have freshly harvested sprouts for Thanksgiving.

Although garden-variety Brussels sprouts are generally smaller than those sold in stores, homegrown sprouts have a sweeter, more nutty flavor. They are a slow-growing vegetable—it takes 90 days or more to reach maturity. Plan to wait until after a few frosts to harvest—a cold snap enhances the flavor, making them milder and sweeter. In mild areas, or if there is deep snow cover, you may be able to harvest Brussels sprouts all winter.

188
PLANT, GROW & HARVEST

SITE Brussels sprouts require a sunny spot, but will grow with a little shade.

BEDMATES Plant with members of the same family—broccoli, cauliflower, and kale.

CARE Easy-care Brussels sprouts need little more than sunshine and regular water to flourish. Pull weeds by hand to avoid damaging the roots or stem.

HOW TO START Because Brussels sprouts take so long to mature, consider starting seeds indoors in early spring. Plant seeds ½ inch (12 mm) deep and 2 inches (5 cm) apart in a seed-starting tray 90 days before last frost date. In spring transplant to the garden.

HARVEST Pick sprouts from the base of the plant upward. Start harvesting when sprouts are 1 to 1½ inches (3–4 cm) in diameter.

PESTS AND DISEASES Brussels sprouts are long-growing, offering lots of opportunity for pest infestation. Repel cutworm damage by adding a cutworm collar around seedlings. Remove aphids with a blast from a garden hose. The biggest pest, however, is cabbage worms. Remove cabbage loopers by hand or use Bt. Control harlequin bugs and flea beetles with appropriate insecticides. Prevent cabbage maggot with diatomaceous earth. And control clubroot and black rot through crop rotation.

189 TAKE THESE TIPS TO THE GARDEN

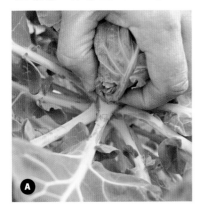

GROW To make Brussels sprouts mature more quickly, remove the growing tip on the top of the plant when the sprouts at the bottom of the stem measure about ½ inch (12 mm) in diameter; harvest sprouts 2 weeks later (A).

SOW OR TRANSPLANT Space plants 24 to 36 inches (61– 91 cm) apart.

HARVEST Pick the lowest sprouts first; keep harvesting up the stem before the leaves yellow (B).

190 KNOW YOUR VARIETIES

'JADE CROSS E HYBRID' An improvement over the old 'Jade Cross Hybrid,' incorporating tolerance of botrytis, a fungal disease, into its characteristics. It matures early and bears dark green sprouts.

'RED RUBINE' An heirloom variety with purplish red sprouts that hold their color even after cooking. It is an attractive alternative to common green varieties.

'BUBBLES' This variety produces round 2-inch (5-cm) flavorful sprouts. Tolerates heat and drought conditions. Harvest 82 days after planting.

'OLIVER' One of the earliest Brussels sprouts to harvest. It has colorful red, purple, and white leaves with ruffled edges.

Brussels sprouts thrive in cool weather and are at peak season from fall to early winter. They taste even sweeter and milder after the first frost.

191
MAKE A SPROUT SLAW

Using a food processor fitted with the slicing blade makes quick work of shaving Brussels sprouts for this citrusy slaw dressed with a green onion vinaigrette.

START TO FINISH: 45 minutes MAKES: 16 servings

8	green onions
½	cup (125 mL) olive oil
½	cup (125 mL) lemon juice
2	tablespoons white wine vinegar
2	tablespoons honey
2	teaspoons ground coriander
2	pounds (1 kg) Brussels sprouts*
4	oranges, peeled and sectioned
1	cup (140 g) cashews, toasted**
1	teaspoon kosher salt

STEP 1 For dressing, chop green onions, keeping white parts separate from green tops. In a blender or food processor combine the white parts of onions, oil, lemon juice, vinegar, honey, and coriander. Cover and blend or process until smooth; set aside.

STEP 2 Trim Brussels sprouts; very thinly slice sprouts.* In an extra-large bowl combine Brussels sprouts and the green tops of onions. Pour dressing over sprouts; toss gently to coat. Add orange sections, cashews, and salt; toss gently to combine.

TO MAKE AHEAD Prepare as directed. Cover and chill up to 4 hours.

*TIP: You may also use a food processor with the slicing blade to shave Brussels sprouts.

**TIP To toast cashews, preheat oven to 350°F (175°C). Spread cashews in a shallow baking pan.

Bake 5 to 10 minutes or until nuts are lightly browned, shaking pan once or twice.

EACH SERVING *162 cal, 11 g fat, 0 mg chol, 140 mg sodium, 15 g carb, 3 g fiber, 4 g pro*

192
GET SWEET ON SPROUTS

As with many vegetables, roasting brings out the best in Brussels sprouts. They get tender and sweet and have browned edges that are irresistible. Apples, dried cherries, and pecans add flavor, color, and crunch to this dish.

PREP: 10 minutes   ROAST: 20 minutes at 425°F (220°C)   MAKES: 4 servings

1   pound (450 g) Brussels sprouts
2   tablespoons olive oil
½   teaspoon kosher salt
⅛   teaspoon cayenne pepper
1   cup (175 g) sliced or coarsely chopped apple
½   cup (80 g) dried cherries or cranberries
¼   cup (27 g) chopped pecans
¼   cup (50 mL) bottled red wine vinaigrette, or desired vinaigrette

STEP 1 Preheat oven to 425°F (220°C). Line a 15×10×1-inch (38×25×2.5-cm) baking pan with foil; set aside. Trim stems and remove any wilted outer leaves from Brussels sprouts. Halve sprouts lengthwise.

STEP 2 Place Brussels sprouts in the prepared baking pan. Drizzle with oil and sprinkle with salt and pepper; toss well to combine.

STEP 3 Roast, uncovered, 15 minutes. Stir in apple, dried cherries, and pecans. Roast, uncovered, 5 to 10 minutes more or until sprouts are crisp-tender and lightly browned. Drizzle with vinaigrette; toss gently to coat.

EACH SERVING *250 cal, 15 g fat, 0 mg chol, 389 mg sodium, 32 g carb, 6 g fiber, 5 g pro*

BEETS

This old-fashioned favorite is becoming trendy once again. More than other vegetables, beets taste of the soil in which they're grown. Beets are cool-weather crops which means there is a harvest in the spring, then, if replanted mid- to- late summer, another harvest in the fall. They can survive frost and almost freezing temperatures, which makes them a good choice for cooler climates.

Beets contain more natural sugar than starch, and roasting in the oven or grilling intensifies the sugar. Beets are a vegetable with two distinctive parts—both the roots and leafy green tops are edible. Usually, leaves are green with veins that match the root color, though some produce reddish-purple leaves and can be prepared much like chard—chopped raw in a salad, sautéed in olive oil with garlic, or braised in broth.

Use beetroots fresh, steamed, or roasted. At room temperature, beetroot is tasty in salads. It's also a favorite for pickling and canning. In addition to red, beetroots may also be yellow, pink, or striped.

193
PLANT, GROW & HARVEST

SITE Plant in a full- to partial-sun location.

BEDMATES Members of the Brassicaceae family, garlic, and mint. Avoid peas, beans, and sage.

CARE Sow seeds directly into loose, well-drained soil when soil temperature is 50°F (10°C). Each seed is actually a fruit containing several seeds; thin when about 2 inches (5 cm) tall to 3 to 4 inches (8–10 cm) between plants. Mulch and water well; beets need plenty of moisture.

HOW TO START Sow beet seeds ½ to 1 inch (1–3 cm) deep and 1 inch (3 cm) apart with rows 1 foot (30 cm) apart. Or scatter beet seeds into a bed, leaving space between each seed to allow for growth. Place a light layer of compost over the top to keep the soil moist.

HARVEST Collect beet greens when they are 4 to 6 inches (10–15 cm) tall. Beetroots can be picked at any time during development, but roots larger than 1 to 2 inches (2.5–5 cm) in diameter tend to be less juicy.

PESTS AND DISEASES Flea beetles feed on young plants; use row covers. Insecticides may be used early in the season but are generally unnecessary in adult plants. Handpick and destroy Mexican bean beetle larvae and beetles. Use insecticide if the problem gets out of control.

194 TAKE THESE TIPS TO THE GARDEN

COLLECT Cut beet greens when they are 4 to 6 inches (10–15 cm) tall (A).

HARVEST Beetroots may be harvested at any time in their growth cycle, but roots larger than 1 to 2 inches (2.5–5 cm) in diameter may become woody.

LEAVE When harvesting beetroots, leave 1 inch (2.5 cm) of foliage on the beet top to prevent the root from "bleeding" during cooking.

195
KNOW YOUR BEET VARIETIES

'BULL'S BLOOD' The deep burgundy foliage of this variety is especially attractive in salads. Its roots develop a candy-stripe interior, ready in 55 days.

'CHIOGGIA' This variety has dark red cylindrical roots, which are ideal for uniform slices of pickled or canned beets.

'GOLDEN' This variety features green leaves, yellow stems, and sweet golden roots. It is ready to harvest in 55 days.

'RED ACE' With round, smooth, deep red roots, this variety is ready to harvest in 55 days.

'RED SANGRIA' This variety offers consistently deep purple-red roots that stay smooth and are ready to harvest in 55 days.

For something completely different, try the Dutch heirloom 'Albino,' which is as white inside and out as its name indicates.

196
USE THE WHOLE BEET

This recipe takes advantage of both root and greens of the plant to make a salad of roasted beets, shredded greens, golden raisins, and pine nuts. Be sure the beet tops are fresh, not wilted.

PREP: 25 minutes   ROAST: 55 minutes at 450°F (230°C)   MAKES: 4 servings

2	pounds (1 kg) fresh beets with tops
2	sprigs fresh rosemary
3	tablespoons olive oil
	Salt and black pepper
½	cup (80 g) golden raisins
2	tablespoons pine nuts, toasted*
4	ounces (115 g) Manchego cheese or ricotta salata, sliced
	Balsamic vinegar (optional)

STEP 1 Preheat oven to 450°F (230°C). Cut tops from beets; set tops aside. Place beets and rosemary on a sheet of heavy foil. Drizzle with 1 tablespoon oil. Bring up two opposite edges of foil; seal with a double fold. Fold in remaining edges to completely enclose. Roast beets in packet about 55 minutes or until tender when pierced with a knife. Carefully open packet to release steam. Set aside until cool enough to handle. Peel skins from beets and cut into wedges. Discard rosemary.

STEP 2 Meanwhile, thoroughly wash and dry beet greens. Discard stalks. Slice any large leaves; leave small leaves whole.

STEP 3 In a large bowl gently toss together warm beets, beet greens, and the remaining 2 tablespoons oil until greens are slightly wilted. Season with salt and pepper.

STEP 4 On a large platter or 4 salad plates arrange beet mixture. Sprinkle with raisins and pine nuts. Top with cheese. If desired, drizzle with balsamic vinegar.

*TIP To toast pine nuts, place them in a small skillet over medium heat. Cook for 2 to 5 minutes or until nuts are lightly browned, stirring often.

EACH SERVING *353 cal, 22 g fat, 25 mg chol, 419 mg sodium, 32 g carb, 5 g fiber, 11 g pro*

197
MAKE A SUPERQUICK BEET SALAD

The beets for this salad are cooked in the microwave for just a few minutes rather than in the oven for almost an hour. When cool, they're sliced and tossed with mixed salad greens, dried cranberries, and a very simple cider vinaigrette.

START TO FINISH: 30 minutes   MAKES: 10 servings

6	small golden and/or red beets, tops trimmed
½	cup (125 mL) cider vinegar
2	tablespoons sugar
2	tablespoons water
¼	cup (50 mL) olive oil
½	teaspoon salt
½	teaspoon black pepper
1	8-ounce (225-g) package mixed salad greens
⅓	cup (38 g) dried cranberries
	Roasted pumpkin seeds (pepitas) (optional)
	Crumbled goat cheese (chèvre) (optional)

STEP 1 Place whole beets in a microwave-safe casserole; add vinegar, sugar, and the water. Microwave, covered, on high 9 to 12 minutes or until beets are tender, stirring once. Remove beets, reserving liquid in casserole. Trim stems and slip off skins. Slice beets; set aside.

STEP 2 For dressing, whisk oil, salt, and pepper into the reserved cooking liquid. In a large bowl toss together beets, salad greens, and cranberries. Pour dressing over salad; toss gently to coat. If desired, sprinkle with pumpkin seeds and cheese.

EACH SERVING *100 cal, 6 g fat, 0 mg chol, 161 mg sodium, 12 g carb, 2 g fiber, 1 g pro*

weldon**owen**

PRESIDENT & PUBLISHER Roger Shaw
SVP, SALES & MARKETING Amy Kaneko

SENIOR EDITOR Lucie Parker
EDITORIAL ASSISTANT Molly Cannon

CREATIVE DIRECTOR Kelly Booth
ART DIRECTOR Lorraine Rath
SENIOR PRODUCTION DESIGNER
   Rachel Lopez Metzger

ASSOCIATE PRODUCTION DIRECTOR
   Michelle Duggan
IMAGING MANAGER Don Hill

Waterbury Publications, Inc., Des Moines, IA
CREATIVE DIRECTOR Ken Carlson
EDITORIAL DIRECTOR Lisa Kingsley
ART DIRECTOR Doug Samuelson
SENIOR EDITOR Tricia Bergman
PRODUCTION ASSISTANT Mindy Samuelson

MEREDITH CORE MEDIA
Editorial Content Director Doug Kouma
Brand Leader Karman Hotchkiss
Creative Director Michelle Bilyeu
BUSINESS ADMINISTRATION
Vice President/Group Publisher Scott Mortimer
Executive Account Director Doug Stark

All images © Meredith Corporation,
with the following exceptions: Shutterstock: 002, 008, 009, 022, 028, 032,
035, 037, 038, 039, 040, 043, 046, 048tb, 051, 056, 078, 118, 123, 138,
141, 144, 156, 174, 179tb, 189, 195

© 2017 Weldon Owen Inc.
1045 Sansome Street, San Francisco, CA 94111
www.weldonowen.com

Weldon Owen is a division of Bonnier Publishing USA.

Library of Congress Control Number is available.

Country Gardens is a registered trademark of Meredith Corporation.

ISBN: 978-1-68188-234-5

10 9 8 7 6 5 4 3 2 1
2017 2018 2019 2020

Printed in China.